"Any good devotional book should do two [ ]
tures, and help us see Christ and our neec [ ]
Murray's *Luke: Stories of Mission and Merc* [ ]
reflection will help individuals, families, : [ ]
more clearly in the Gospel of Luke as they read the text and see Jesus
more and more in all the Scriptures. May the Lord use it to encourage
many to read and understand Luke's Gospel in a deeper way."

Chris Bruno, Global Partner for Hawaii and the Pacific Islands,
Training Leaders International; Pastor, Kailua Baptist Church;
author, *The Whole Story of the Bible in 16 Verses*

"In fifty daily five-minute devotionals, David Murray manages to pack
the transforming power of the gospel into bite-sized pieces that can
change readers' lives. If you are ready to get to know God and yourself
better on a simple, concise, but profound journey through the story
of Jesus in Luke, this resource is going to be an enormous blessing
to you! David doesn't shy away from tougher subjects like death and
temptation, and he handles them so pastorally that you can't help but
walk away encouraged."

Adam Griffin, Lead Pastor, Eastside Community Church,
Dallas, Texas; coauthor, *Family Discipleship*

The StoryChanger Devotional Series

By David Murray

Luke: Stories of Mission and Mercy

Luke

Luke

Stories of Mission and Mercy

David Murray

WHEATON, ILLINOIS

Library of Congress Cataloging-in-Publication Data

Names: Murray, David, 1966 May 28– author.

Title: Luke : stories of mission and mercy / David Murray.

Description: Wheaton, Illinois : Crossway, [2022] | Series: StoryChanger devotionals | Includes bibliographical references.

Identifiers: LCCN 2021059489 (print) | LCCN 2021059490 (ebook) | ISBN 9781433580895 (trade paperback) | ISBN 9781433580901 (pdf) | ISBN 9781433580918 (mobi) | ISBN 9781433580925 (epub)

Subjects: LCSH: Bible. Luke—Devotional literature. | Bible. Luke—Criticism, interpretation, etc. | Mission of the church—Biblical teaching. | Mercy—Biblical teaching.

Classification: LCC BS2595.54 .M87 2022 (print) | LCC BS2595.54 (ebook) | DDC 226.4/06—dc23/eng/20220224

LC record available at https://lccn.loc.gov/2021059489

LC ebook record available at https://lccn.loc.gov/2021059490

Crossway is a publishing ministry of Good News Publishers.

VP		31	30	29	28	27	26	25	24	23	22
15	14	13	12	11	10	9	8	7	6	5	4	3	2	1

Dedicated to David Faasse,
my wise mentor, my constant
encourager, and, above
all, my beloved friend.

Contents

Introduction to the StoryChanger Devotionals

Do you want to know the Bible's Story better, but don't know how? Do you want to change your story, but don't know how? Do you want to share the Bible's Story and the way it has changed your story, but don't know how? The StoryChanger Devotional series is the answer to this triple *how*.

How can I know the Bible better? At different points in my Christian life, I've tried to use various helps to go deeper in personal Bible study, but I found commentaries were too long and technical, whereas study Bibles were too brief and not practical.

How can I change my life for the better? I knew the Bible's Story was meant to change my story but couldn't figure out how to connect God's Story with my story in a transformative way. I was stuck, static, and frustrated at my lack of change, growth, and progress.

How can I share God's Story better? I've often been embarrassed by how slow and ineffective I am at sharing God's Story one-on-one. I know God's Story relates to other people's stories and that God's Story can change others' stories for the better, but I'm reluctant to seek out opportunities and hesitant when they arise.

So how about a series of books that teach us the Bible's Story in a way that helps to change our story and equips us to tell the Story to others. Or, to put it another way, how about books that teach us God's Story in a way that changes ours and others' stories?

After writing *The StoryChanger: How God Rewrites Our Story by Inviting Us into His* as an introduction to Jesus as the transformer of our stories, I thought, "Okay, what now? That's the theory, what about the practice? That's the introduction, but what about the next chapters? Jesus is the StoryChanger, but how can his Story change my story in practical ways on a daily basis? And how do I share his life-changing Story with others?"

I looked for daily devotionals that would take me through books of the Bible in a way that explained God's Story, changed my story, and equipped me to tell God's Story to others in a life-changing way. When I couldn't find any resources that had all three elements, I thought, "I'll write some devotionals for myself to help me know God's Story, change my story, and tell the story to others."

A few weeks later COVID hit, and I decided to start sharing these devotionals with the congregation I was serving at the time. I wanted to keep them connected with God and one another through that painful period of prolonged isolation from church and from one another.

I found that, like myself, people seemed to be hungry for daily devotionals that were more than emotional. They enjoyed daily devotionals that were educational, transformational, and missional. We worked our way verse-by-verse through books of the Bible with a focus on brevity, simplicity, clarity, practicality, and shareability. The StoryChanger started changing our stories with his Story, turning us into storytellers and therefore storychangers too.

Although these devotionals will take only about five minutes a day, I'm not promising you quick fixes. No, the StoryChanger usually changes our stories little by little. But over months and years of exposure to the StoryChanger's Story, he rewrites our story, and, through us, rewrites others' stories too.

To encourage you, I invite you to join the StoryChangers community at www.thestorychanger.life. There you can sign up for the weekly StoryChangers newsletter and subscribe to the StoryChangers podcast. Let's build a community of storychangers, committed Christians who dedicate themselves to knowing God's Story better, being changed by God's Story for the better, and sharing God's Story better. We'll meet the StoryChanger, have our stories changed, and become storychangers. I look forward to meeting you there and together changing stories with God's Story.[1]

---

1 Some of this content originally appeared on the *Living the Bible* podcast, which has since been replaced by *The StoryChanger* podcast, https://podcasts.apple.com/us /podcast/the-storychanger/id1581826891.

Introduction to *Luke: Stories of Mission and Mercy*

Luke wrote his Gospel to introduce his readers, especially Gentile readers, to Jesus. Luke was a physician, so we're not surprised that his account emphasizes Christ's double mission of suffering *with* others in sympathy and his suffering *for* others to heal them. Story after story shows us Jesus's love and compassion for sick sinners, and Luke's Gospel gradually moves deeper and deeper into Christ's suffering for sick sinners. We see mission and mercy in Jesus's mission of mercy.

Although there are fifty daily devotionals in this book, we will not cover every story or passage in Luke's Gospel. The passages I've omitted are repeated in one of the other three Gospels and will be covered in the other StoryChanger Devotionals.[1] Once you have read all four devotionals on the Gospels, you will have covered the whole Gospel story.

May these stories of mission and mercy change our stories so that we continue Christ's mission and mercy in the world.

---

1 You'll find a table showing which Gospel passages are covered by each daily devotional at www.thestorychanger.life/gospels.

Confidence in the Scriptures builds confidence in our salvation.

Hear
God's Story | Change
Your Story | Tell
the Story | Change
Others' Stories

1

Soul Sandpaper for a Smooth Finish

LUKE 1:1–23

Why does God sometimes sandpaper our souls? Because preparation perfects painting. Painters spend five times longer preparing a surface than painting it because the better the preparation, the better the paint looks and lasts. If that's true for making a surface beautiful, how much more for making a soul beautiful? Although it can be excruciating, soul preparation is vital for soul perfection. If we want a perfect salvation that looks good and lasts long, then we must prepare for some painful sandpapering.

How should we respond when our heavenly painter prepares us for perfection? Let's visit the perfect painter's workshop in Luke 1:1–17.

Preparation Requires Careful Records 1:1–4

When I read a biography, I'm not interested in the author's qualifications or research methods. I just want to get into the story, leaving technical details to the scholars. But we can't do that when it comes to something as important as the biography of Jesus Christ. Unless we're convinced that the Gospel record has been carefully prepared, that it is true and accurate, our faith will not last long or look good.

That's why Luke began his biography of Jesus by assuring us of how carefully he prepared his account: "It seemed good to me also, having followed all things closely for some time past, to write an orderly account for you, most excellent Theophilus, that you may have certainty concerning the things you have been taught" (1:3–4).

God prepares us for soul perfection by persuading us of the Bible's perfection.

Confidence in the Scriptures builds confidence in our salvation.

What do these perfect records reveal about soul preparation?

Preparation Requires Convicting Repentance 1:5–23

My son, Allan, has a painting business, and he has shown me what happens if he paints without sandpapering first. The paint doesn't stick, or, if it does, it looks awful. Allan hates sandpapering because it's long, hard, dusty, sweaty, and exhausting work; but he loves the results—painted surfaces that look great and last long.

God sent John the Baptist to sandpaper people, to rough them up, to convict them of sin, so that when Jesus came with his salvation, it would stick, look great, and last long. John was a sandpaper man with a sandpaper ministry who would "make ready for the Lord a people prepared" (1:17).

This unique preparatory task required a uniquely prepared character. God turned John the Baptist into a great man because he was going to turn a great many to God (1:15–17). No wonder God said to his parents, "You will have joy and gladness, and many will rejoice at his birth" (1:14). Sandpapering isn't glamorous work, but it is great work.

Zechariah doubted God's word and therefore was silenced by God until John's birth (1:18–23). Zechariah was unprepared for the preparer, so God prepared him more thoroughly by disabling the tongue that doubted God's promise. The Lord compassionately sandpapered him with discipline to perfect him.

Submit to spiritual sandpaper for a smooth soul.

Changing Our Story with God's Story

In my childhood story Bibles, John the Baptist always looked ugly and rough. I especially disliked his disgusting locust sandwiches. However, in my early twenties, God brought a couple of John the Baptist type ministers into my life (minus the locusts). They convinced me of the reliability of the Bible and sandpapered my soul with conviction of sin until I was ready for the smooth finish of salvation. I didn't enjoy these painful months, but they prepared me for a salvation that stuck better and looked better. When God wants to change our story, he starts with spiritual sandpaper. It doesn't feel good, but it sure looks good when he's done.

Summary: How should we respond when our heavenly painter prepares us for perfection? *Submit to biblical truth and spiritual sandpaper for a smooth and beautiful finish.*

Question: When God sandpapers you, what helps you to submit rather than resist?

Prayer: Heavenly Painter, use your word to prepare me for Jesus and sand me so that your salvation sticks forever and looks better. Amen.

God chooses the smallest people for the biggest jobs.

Hear
God's Story

Change
Your Story

Tell
the Story

Change
Others' Stories

2

Climbing Mount Impossible

LUKE 1:26–38

If life were a movie, we could title it *Mission Impossible*. We face impossible situations, challenges, decisions, problems, and temptations. Unlike Tom Cruise, we feel so small and scared when facing such impossible challenges. *How can small people like us overcome mountainous challenges?*

In Luke 1:26–38, God charted a road over Mount Impossible for fearful Mary. Let's follow in her footsteps so we can summit the Everests in our own lives.

God Gives Big Jobs to Small People 1:26–29

God commissioned the angel Gabriel to tell Mary, an uneducated nobody from a nothing town, that she would be the Savior's mother. The lowest was to carry the highest. What powerful pity!

How does an angel say hello? "Greetings, O favored one, the Lord is with you!" (1:28). "Favored one" means a passive recipient of God's grace. "The Lord is with you" was a frequent angelic encouragement when someone faced an enormous challenge. Little wonder that Mary "was greatly troubled at the saying, and tried to discern what sort of greeting this might be" (1:29).

God chooses the smallest people for the biggest jobs.

How can such small people do such big jobs for God?

God Gives Big Promises to Small People 1:30–33

Seeing Mary's shock, Gabriel assured her: "Do not be afraid, Mary, for you have found favor with God. And behold, you will conceive in your womb and bear a son, and you shall call his name Jesus" (1:30–31). So far, so (relatively) normal: conception, birth, naming. This son would be Mary's son.

But then things take off and go into orbit. "He will be great and will be called the Son of the Most High. And the Lord God will give to him the throne of his father David, and he will reign over the house of Jacob forever, and of his kingdom there will be no end" (1:32–33). Now we're into another realm and dimension altogether. This is far from normal, far from human. This wasn't just Mary's son; this was God's Son.

God makes big promises and keeps the smallest details.

But big promises also need big faith!

God Gives Big Faith to Small People 1:34–38

"And Mary said to the angel, 'How will this be, since I am a virgin?'" (1:34). This was not doubt or skepticism, but faith seeking understanding. She wasn't questioning the *what*; she was asking about the *how*.

Gabriel explained that the Holy Spirit would come upon her. Just as the Holy Spirit hovered over the original creation to bring everything out of nothing at the beginning, so he would also hover over Mary's womb to bring the Savior out of nothing and give the world a new beginning (1:35). To encourage Mary's faith, Gabriel pointed out that God had given the aged and barren Elizabeth a child, for "nothing will be impossible with God" (1:36–37).

Mary said, "Behold, I am the servant of the Lord; let it be to me according to your word" (1:38). God gives big faith to enable big surrenders.

It's impossible to find impossible *in God's vocabulary.*

Changing Our Story with God's Story

All of us have an outer story all can read, and an inner story only we can read. Like most of you, when I face great challenges or opportunities, my inner voice can get stuck on repeat: "It's impossible . . . it's impossible . . ."—paralyzing me with fatalistic fear. But thankfully I've also experienced how God's Story can change my inner story and therefore my outer story too.

May this Gospel story about Jesus's entry into the world enter our hearts and change our inner voice to: "Nothing will be impossible with God . . . nothing will be impossible with God . . ." These words shrink Mount Impossible into a molehill and transform small, scared doubters into strong, steady climbers.

Summary: How can small people like us overcome mountainous challenges? *Trust our big God to do big things in, for, and through small people.*

Question: Do you know people who are facing Mount Impossible today? How will you help them start climbing with this message?

Prayer: Lord of Impossibilities, I bring my impossibilities to you. Change my impossible story to show that nothing is impossible with you. Amen.

Joy, joy, joy 'cause Jesus, Jesus, Jesus.

 Hear God's Story | Change Your Story | Tell the Story | Change Others' Stories

3

Jumping for Jesus

LUKE 1:39–56

Our hearts can jump higher than our legs. Joy jumps heights the longest legs will never reach. How high did our hearts jump when we graduated, when we got married, when our first child was born, and when we caught our biggest salmon? Joy jumps are record-breaking jumps.

But you might be thinking, "My heart is broken, my spirit is heavy, and my shoulders are weighed down with the weight of the world. I can hardly stand up, never mind jump up." *How can we jump for joy when we are jaded?* In Luke 1:39–56, Mary, Elizabeth, and John the baby team up to teach us how to jump for joy again.

Jesus-Joy Is Jumping Joy 1:39–45

When two first-time moms meet, the only subject is babies, babies, babies. How much more so when one mom-to-be is a teen and the other, her aunt, is sixty-plus. Even Elizabeth's unborn baby joined in, leaping for joy in her womb at the sound of Mary's greeting (1:41). The baby didn't just kick; he somehow managed to leap. Quite the bouncing baby! John was so excited, he could hardly wait to get out of the womb and serve Jesus.

The same Holy Spirit that somersaulted John also animated Elizabeth with spiritual joy as she exclaimed [to Mary] with a loud cry, "Blessed are you among women, and blessed is the fruit of your womb! . . . And blessed is she who believed that there would be a fulfillment of what was spoken to her from the Lord" (1:42, 45). Blessed, blessed, blessed! Triply blessed.

Joy, joy, joy 'cause Jesus, Jesus, Jesus.

Why is Jesus such a joy-fuel? Let's ask Mary.

Mighty Mercy Is Giant Joy 1:46–56

Mary joined this festival of joy with a joyful song that magnified the Lord, not herself, and rejoiced in her salvation, not her sinlessness:

> My soul magnifies the Lord,
>> and my spirit rejoices in God my Savior. (1:46–47)

Elizabeth had expressed wonder that Mary, the mother of her Lord, would visit her (1:43), but instead of claiming any merit medals for this, Mary sang of God's mighty mercy:

> He who is mighty has done great things for me,
>> and holy is his name.
> And his mercy is for those who fear him
>> from generation to generation. (1:49–50)

Her theme song showcases mighty mercy, not Mary's merit. She exults not just in God's might alone, and not just in God's mercy alone, but in God's might and mercy together. A mercy that can actually do something. A mercy that can do everything. A mercy that's not just a pitiful feeing but a powerful force. Mary describes God's mighty mercy in action:

> He has shown strength with his arm;
>> he has scattered the proud in the thoughts of their hearts;
> he has brought down the mighty from their thrones
>> and exalted those of humble estate;

he has filled the hungry with good things,
and the rich he has sent away empty.
He has helped his servant Israel,
in remembrance of his mercy. (1:51–54)

Mighty mercy makes many merry.

Changing Our Story with God's Story

I would hate to be saved by my merit, even if it were possible. Why? Because it wouldn't make me half as happy as being saved by God's mercy. There's something about being gifted salvation that makes it far more enjoyable than an earned salvation, isn't there? Most joys lose their initial energy and our joy-jumps get shorter. But Jesus-joy and mighty mercy spring us higher and higher. We jump higher with age and, even when we die, we will jump all the way into heaven's joys and never stop for all eternity.

Summary: How can we jump for joy when we are jaded? *Use Jesus-joy and mighty mercy to put new springs in your soul.*

Question: How will you use Jesus-joy and mighty mercy to jump higher today?

Prayer: Joy-Giver, my soul is sad and sagging. Change my story by putting a new spring in my step with Jesus-joy and mighty mercy. Amen.

Perfect promises require a perfect promiser.

4

The Only
Promise Keeper

LUKE 1:57–80

Broken promises break people. Whether it's wedding promises, business promises, investment promises, privacy promises, or political promises—when promises are broken, people are broken too. Broken promises break marriages, companies, finances, friendships, nations, and health. Broken promises break us, but kept promises build us up.

Can we find a perfect promiser with perfect promises to build better lives? In Luke 1:57–80, the Holy Spirit opened Zechariah's mouth to point us to the perfect promiser with perfect promises.

The God of Promises Is the Perfect Promiser

The Holy Spirit silenced Zechariah for many months because he doubted God's promises of a special son. But we know that his months of enforced silence gave him time to ponder his unbelief and doubt because, when he eventually spoke, his first words were about God's truthfulness and trustworthiness. We can imagine Zechariah reading his Old Testament and, using four different colors, underlining and highlighting passages that revealed God as the perfect promiser:

- God will raise up a Savior "as he spoke by the mouth of his holy prophets from of old" (1:70).
- God will show "the mercy promised to our fathers" (1:72).
- God will "remember his holy covenant" (1:72).
- God will keep "the oath that he swore to our father Abraham" (1:73).

Look at the words Zechariah used to describe God's word: *holy prophecies, promises, covenant,* and *oath.* Layer upon layer of accuracy, certainty, veracity, credibility, and authenticity. That's a mortar that will withstand spiritual bombs, hurricanes, earthquakes, and wars. When everything else is flattened, the divine promiser is unmoved and unmovable.

Perfect promises require a perfect promiser.

So, what are our perfect God's perfect promises?

The Promises of God Are Perfect Promises

Zechariah not only listed God's confident characteristics, but he also listed God's confident commitments. Consider how massive each of these Old Testament promises were and how God kept them:

- I will visit and redeem you. Promise kept (1:68; see Isa. 54:7–17).
- I will send a powerful salvation to you. Promise kept (1:69; see 1 Sam. 2:10).
- I will save you from your enemies. Promise kept (1:71; see Isa. 14:1–3).
- I will show you mercy. Promise kept (1:72; see Ezek. 16:8).
- I will deliver you to serve God without fear. Promise kept (1:74; see Zeph. 3:15–17).
- I will give you knowledge of salvation. Promise kept (1:77; see Jer. 31:34).
- I will forgive your sins in my tender mercy. Promise kept (1:77–78; see Jer. 31:34).
- I will give you light in deathly darkness. Promise kept (1:79; see Isa. 60:1–3).
- I will guide your feet into the way of peace. Promise kept (1:79; see Isa. 42:16).

We couldn't keep one of these promises, yet God kept all nine of them in Jesus. As Paul said, "All the promises of God find their Yes in him" (2 Cor. 1:20). These perfect promises were made by a perfect God and were perfectly kept through his perfect Son.

We're perfect promise breakers, but Christ is the perfect promise keeper.

Changing Our Story with God's Story

Let's confess that we've broken our promises to God and others. Our broken promises have broken people and even broken ourselves. Let's look away from our stories of broken promises and look to God's Story of kept promises to build a stable life and a safe eternity. We'll never be saved by our promises to God but only by his promises to us.

"But others have broken promises to me and broken me in the process," you protest. Me too. I've been broken by broken promises. I've grown skeptical and cynical at times, finding it hard to trust anyone.

But Jesus understands even better because he is the promised one who was broken in pieces by some of the people he gave his promises to. Yet, no matter how much hell and earth threw at the promise keeper, he kept all his promises. Don't doubt him, but instead totally trust him.

Summary: Can we find a perfect promiser with perfect promises to build better lives? *Build your life upon the God of the promises and the promises of God.*

Question: Which promise of God will you rest on and build on today?

Prayer: Promise Maker and Promise Keeper, I confess that I have doubted you and your promises. Help me to stop building my life with straw and instead build my life with the granite promises of the perfect promiser. Amen.

The devil says,
"Sin to be happy,"
but God says,
"Sing to be happy."

5

Join the World's Greatest Choir

LUKE 2:8–20

Happiness makes us sing, but singing also makes us happy. How so? Studies have discovered that the deep breathing in singing brings more oxygen into the blood, releasing feel-good chemicals in the brain. Also, the concentration required in singing distracts us from our problems and therefore reduces our stress. Singing in a choir is even better because the social connection and cooperation with others give us a lift. *So, what songs should we sing to maximize our happiness?*

Let's listen to the angel choir in Luke 2:8–14. They are the best-ever choir, singing the best-ever lyrics of the best-ever song in the best-ever way.

God Is Our Song Leader 2:8–14

Shepherds were watching their flock in a field near Bethlehem when an angel appeared to them and the glory of the Lord shone all around them (2:8–9). At first the shepherds were afraid, but the angel announced "good news of great joy . . . for all the people" (2:10). This great news about a great Savior started a great choir singing a great song (2:10–14).

When Jesus was born, God told all the angels to stop what they were doing and devote their whole beings to worshiping this baby (Heb. 1:6). If God called sinless angels to worship a Savior they didn't need, how much more does he call sinners like us to worship a Savior we desperately need?

The devil says, "Sin to be happy," but God says, "Sing to be happy."

Who wrote this angelic song?

God Is Our Songwriter 2:14

God intended this song to be sung in divine stereo, with one speaker pointed toward God in heaven and one toward people on earth. Heaven's speaker blared "Glory to God" (2:14). The angels had praised God many times, but never like this, never so many at once, never at such volume, because never had they so much reason to praise. Earth's speaker broadcast "Peace to people" (2:14). Glory up to God, peace down to people. Glory reaching higher than ever before, and peace reaching lower than ever before.

God's glory is to give us peace, and our peace gives God glory.

What is this song about?

God Is Our Song 2:15–20

God led the song, wrote the song, was the audience for the song, and was the subject of the song. The angels were singing to him about him. The happy news made them happy angels with a happy song that spread happiness to the world.

The lowly shepherds had the best seats at the best concert ever. When it finished, they had to find the Savior the angels were singing about. With angel songs ringing in their ears, they found Jesus, told Mary and Joseph and anyone else who would listen about the concert, then returned, glorifying and praising God for all they had heard and seen. Angel songs produced shepherd songs.

Singing about God sparks speaking about God.

Changing Our Story with God's Story

Jesus brings more glory to God and more peace to earth than anyone else. Like the angels he prioritized glory to God so that he could give peace to people. When we aim at God's glory first and most in our worship, God will bring his peace into our hearts through worship. Glory up to God, peace down to people, then witness out to the world. When we have truly worshiped, we will truly witness. When our souls have been stirred, our mouths will be stirred. The true gauge of whether we've worshiped in spirit and truth is whether we then witness to the truth by the Spirit.

Summary: What songs should we sing to maximize our happiness? *Lift up praise songs to lift up God, lift up your spirit, and lift up your witness.*

Question: Which Christian song helps you to lift up God, your spirit, and your witness?

Prayer: Most High, Most Holy, and Most Happy God, I lift you high with holy and happy songs. Lift me high with holy and happy singing. Amen.

Our hope of life after death is Christ's life and death.

6

A Baby Who Helps Us to Die

LUKE 2:21–35

There are millions of books on how to live, but very few on how to die. Lots of people want to teach us how to postpone death through healthy living, but very few teach on how to face up to death when healthy living is fading. Even if we do summon up the courage to talk about death, who can we trust on the subject? There aren't exactly many people who can speak with experience about how to die. *Many can help us to live, but who can help us to die?*

In Luke 2:21–38, we meet a dying man, Simeon, cuddling a newborn baby that helped him to die. What was it about the new life of baby Jesus that gave Simeon a new view of death?

Jesus Helps Us Die with His Peace 2:29–31

When Jesus's parents took him to the temple to present him to the Lord, God arranged for them to meet an old, Spirit-filled believer named Simeon. God had promised Simeon that he would see the Savior before he died, and the Lord led him by the Spirit to meet Jesus that day. When Simeon saw Jesus, he took him up in his arms, blessed God, and said,

> Lord, now you are letting your servant depart in peace,
>   according to your word;
> for my eyes have seen your salvation
>   that you have prepared in the presence of all peoples.
>   (2:29–31)

As soon as he saw Jesus's new life, he had a new view of his death. When he saw the Savior, he saw his own salvation. He could depart in peace because Jesus had given him peace.

Jesus's birth helps us to die.

What about the darkness of death?

Jesus Helps Us Die with His Light 2:32

Death is dark. It's a gloomy experience for the dying one and for the loved ones. What comes after is dim and mysterious. Why do we have to die? What's the purpose of death? What's next? It's murky, shadowy, somber.

But not for Simeon. Seeing Jesus turned the lights on. He could depart in peace because Jesus was "a light for revelation to the Gentiles, / and for glory to your people Israel" (2:32). Simeon identified the bright glory cloud that shepherded Israel through the wilderness in the Old Testament as the Son of God he was snuggling in his arms. What was cloud and fire was now flesh and blood. That light of Israel was now being revealed to the Gentiles as well. Jesus replaced the darkness of ignorance, doubt, and depression with the light of knowledge, assurance, and confidence. We now know what's happening in death, what's after death, and where we're going in death.

Jesus turns on the grave light.

If that's the role of Christ's birth, what about his death?

Jesus Helps Us Die with His Death 2:34-35

Although Jesus came to turn the lights on, many wanted to turn his light off. Simeon predicted that, despite saving others from death, Jesus himself would be put to death. "Behold, this child is appointed for the fall and rising of many in Israel, and for a sign that is opposed (and a sword will pierce through your own soul also), so that thoughts from many hearts may be revealed" (2:34–35). Simeon looked at this precious baby and saw that a sword would pierce not only his mother's heart, but his own soul too. However, this sharp blade would separate not only the fibers of his flesh, but also people, by revealing who they truly are before God.

Our hope of life after death is Christ's life and death.

Changing Our Story with God's Story

Jesus changed the end of Simeon's story, and he can change the end of our stories too. If we hold Jesus in our arms by faith, we can face death with confidence and live with anticipation of heavenly peace.

Summary: Who can help us to die? *Cuddle Jesus's life and death by faith, for help to live and die with peace and joy.*

Question: How will this view of death change the way you feel today?

Prayer: Death-Destroyer, I thank you for transforming my death with your peace, your light, and your death. I embrace you by faith in life and in death, knowing that you will meet me on the other side, holding me in your arms.

Jesus understood
God's word best
because he was
God's best Word.

7

How to Parent the Perfect Child

LUKE 2:39–52

Parenting is rougher and tougher than plumbing. Talk about a "dirty job"! Sometimes we get into such a mess, we ask ourselves, "What's the point of all this stress? *What's the purpose of parenting?*" Luke answers with a description of Jesus in Luke 2:39–52. "And the child grew and became strong, filled with wisdom. And the favor of God was upon him. . . . And Jesus increased in wisdom and in stature and in favor with God and man" (2:40, 52). To have our children described like that would be a dream, wouldn't it? What made Jesus such a perfect child?

Jesus Loved the Church 2:41–46

After eight days of intense Passover rituals, most twelve-year-old boys would be longing to get home to their friends. But while his parents headed home, unknown to them, Jesus stayed behind in the temple. A day later, his parents realized Jesus was missing and returned to search for him. After three terrifying days of frantic searching, they found him in the temple engaging with the religious teachers. Why didn't they look there first? Probably they just never thought that after eight days of church, any boy would want more church! But Jesus wasn't just any boy. He loved the church and couldn't get enough of church.

Jesus loved the temple because he was the temple.

What did Jesus do there? He studied.

Jesus Loved Learning 2:46–47

"They found him in the temple, sitting among the teachers, listening to them and asking them questions. And all who heard him were amazed at his understanding and his answers" (2:46–47). Jesus loved learning, especially about himself. This was his first opportunity to learn under the best Bible teachers in the country. He listened intently and asked multiple questions. What amazed the observers was not the teachers, but the student! He began by listening and questioning, but ended up teaching and answering. Three days to graduate from pre-K to PhD; that's my kind of school!

Jesus understood God's word best because he was God's best Word.

What did he learn about? His mission.

Jesus Loved His Mission 2:48–49

Although Joseph and Mary were astonished at what they saw, they were more concerned with all the stress of their search. But Jesus responded, "Why were you looking for me? Did you not know that I must be in my Father's house?" (2:49). He was saying, "If you really knew me, you wouldn't have wasted your time searching the city for three days. You would have come straight here. I must be in my Father's house because I'm on mission for my Father. I came to his house for his instructions."

Jesus didn't come to play with friends, but to save sinners.

So, did Jesus ignore his parents? No, he submitted to them.

Jesus Loved His Parents 2:50–51

Jesus understood himself better than Joseph and Mary did. But they were still his parents, and therefore "he went down with them and came to Nazareth and was submissive to them" (2:51). He loved them enough to teach them, and he loved God enough to submit to them.

Mary and Joseph were imperfect parents of the perfect child.

Changing Our Story with God's Story

None of us can raise the perfect child, because there only was one, Jesus Christ. Yes, we aim to have children who increase in wisdom and stature and in favor with God and men. And yes, we plan to have children who love the church, love learning, love mission, and love their parents. But our aims and our plans fall and fail every single day. Our hope is not in our perfect parenting or our perfect children, but in God's perfect parenting of his perfect Son. As failing parents and faulty children, we look to the perfect Savior to cover all our faults and failings.

Summary: What's the purpose of parenting? *As imperfect parents and imperfect children, we look to Jesus to look like Jesus.*

Question: How will this passage improve your relationship with your parents, your children, and your Savior?

Prayer: Perfect Parent, I thank you for your perfect Son. Because I am an imperfect parent with imperfect children, help me to raise my children to look to Jesus and look like Jesus.

Our Father's forgiveness is full, free, fast, final, and forever.

 Hear God's Story | Change Your Story | Tell the Story | Change Others' Stories

8

The Greatest Answer to the Greatest Question

LUKE 3:1-14

"Half of these patients are here because of unresolved guilt." That's what a consultant psychiatrist told a doctor friend of mine as they walked through a mental health facility. "They need forgiveness," he explained, "and I can't help them with that." The consultant, who wasn't a Christian, cared deeply for his patients, but felt hopeless and helpless when confronted with the deepest human problem: *"How can I get forgiveness?"* Sadly, a few years later, this psychiatrist committed suicide. He knew the greatest question but didn't know the greatest answer. Let's hear God's answer through the ministry of John the Baptist in Luke 3:1-14.

Repentance Produces Forgiveness 3:1-6

John the Baptist began his desert ministry by "proclaiming a baptism of repentance for the forgiveness of sins" (3:3). Out of all the hundreds of possible biblical topics, he chose forgiveness through repentance. It didn't matter what day of the week, what hour of the day, or who his audience was, his sermon was the same: forgiveness through repentance. John went to the heart of the matter, the greatest human need: How can I get forgiveness? How can I get my sins cancelled, washed away, removed, forgotten?

Like the psychiatrist, John saw how much damage unresolved guilt did to men and women, especially to their relationship with God. But, unlike the psychiatrist, John had the answer: forgiveness through repentance. He offered God's full, free, fast, final, and forever forgiveness through repentance. Repentance resulted in remission. Repentance opened the floodgates of forgiveness (3:4–6). Human repentance is the only gateway to God's forgiveness, but that gate is available and accessible to all.

Our Father's forgiveness is full, free, fast, final, and forever.

So, how do I know if I've repented?

Repentance Produces Fruit 3:7–14

John demanded demanding repentance. He saw the danger of people thinking that repentance was simply saying sorry, but continuing to sin. He feared that many wanted their sins forgiven but didn't want their sin finished. Some wanted to flee God's anger, but not what made him angry (3:7). Hence John's insistence that they "bear fruits in keeping with repentance" (3:8).

Repentance isn't just saying sorry; it's *being* sorry. It's not just a change of mind but also a change of heart. It's not just canceling the past; it's changing the future. It's not just washing our past; it's washing our person. This is why John joined baptism with his message of repentance. This picture and his preaching said one thing: repentance removes sin's penalty and sin's presence. Repentance produces a clean record and a clean life. The test of forgiveness is your fruit not your father (3:8).

How quickly did John expect to see that fruit? God's forgiveness was so powerful that he expected immediate fruit: "Even now the axe is laid to the root of the trees. Every tree therefore that does not bear good fruit is cut down and thrown into the fire" (3:9). Where did John expect to see most fruit? In the areas people sinned the most (3:10–14). Full forgiveness is always popular, but fruitful repentance is usually lonely.

Everyone wants forgiveness, but few want repentance.

Changing Our Story with God's Story

Nothing changed my life like forgiveness. By my early twenties, I had tried everything to change my life, but nothing succeeded for long. I had unresolved guilt that was causing me deep depression and terrifying anxiety. Sins from my past haunted me, and sins in my present harassed me. What could break the power of my sin and my guilt? Christ's forgiveness did it.

How can removing the penalty for sin remove our passion for sin? I'm not 100 percent sure how that works psychologically, but it definitely works spiritually. Guilt propagates flesh, but forgiveness cultivates fruit. The more we grasp forgiveness, the more we repent of sin, the more we produce good fruit, the more we grasp forgiveness, and so on. What a virtuous cycle! Absolution is the solution.

Summary: How can I get forgiveness? *Repent for full, free, fast, final, and forever forgiveness.*

Question: What feelings and fruit flow from forgiveness in your life?

Prayer: Forgiver of Wrong, make me fruitful in right.

Jesus was unashamed to identify with us, so let's be unashamed to identify with him.

9

Three Baptisms

LUKE 3:15-22

Baptism befuddles believers. Few topics confuse Christians as much as baptism. Whether one is talking about infant baptism or believer's baptism, many believe that the waters of baptism are saving. So let me state this as clearly as possible. Baptism does not save. So, *what does baptism do?* If anyone should know what baptism stands for, it's John the Baptist. Let's ask him by examining his ministry in Luke 3:15-21.

Jesus Cleanses Us with the Baptism of the Holy Spirit 3:15-16

How good was John the Baptist at his job of preparing the people for Jesus? "The people were waiting expectantly and were all wondering in their hearts if John might possibly be the Messiah" (3:15 NIV). Mission accomplished! This is exactly where John wanted them: waiting expectantly and wondering excitedly.

But John hated having people's eyes upon him. So began the second phase of his ministry, pointing away from himself to Jesus. "John answered them all, saying, 'I baptize you with water. But he who is mightier than I is coming, the strap of whose sandals I am not worthy to untie. He will baptize you with the Holy Spirit and fire'" (3:16).

John wants us to know that Jesus is superior to him in three ways: Jesus is more powerful than John, he's more prestigious than John (John is not worthy to untie Jesus's sandals), and he's a greater purifier than John (Jesus will baptize you with the Holy Spirit). Jesus performs what the water pictures.

Don't settle for mere water baptism, when you can also have Spirit baptism.

What's the consequence of mere water baptism and no Spirit baptism?

John Warns Us about the Baptism of Fire 3:16-17

Holy Spirit baptism isn't an optional extra that God gives to only the most committed Christians. It's a nonnegotiable gift for all Christians. Without Spirit baptism we get fire baptism. "He will baptize you with . . . fire. His winnowing fork is in his hand, to clear his threshing floor and to gather the wheat into his barn, but the chaff he will burn with unquenchable fire" (3:16–17). If we're not baptized by the Holy Spirit, we'll be burned with his holy fire.[1]

Only Spirit baptism can extinguish fire baptism.

But Jesus was baptized too. Why?

Jesus Identifies with Us in His Baptism of Water 3:18-22

"With many other exhortations [John] preached good news to the people" (3:18). He exhorted the people to flee fire baptism and proclaimed the good news of Spirit baptism. But then Jesus appeared and proclaimed the good news by being baptized himself. Jesus the baptizer was baptized. Why? He didn't need to be cleansed. He didn't need to repent. The answer is in these words: "When all the people were being baptized, Jesus was baptized too" (3:21 NIV). The people were baptized, therefore Jesus was baptized. The first act of

---

1 Some commentators view the fire as a positive cleansing of God's people (Isa. 4:2–5), in which case the winnowing metaphor represents the coming of Christ's kingdom in this world.

his ministry was to identify with sinners, to be numbered with the transgressors (Isa. 53:12). He wasn't a sinner, but identified with sinners. What tender pity!

God himself loved this sight, because, as Jesus prayed in and over his baptism, "the heavens were opened, and the Holy Spirit descended on him in bodily form, like a dove; and a voice came from heaven, 'You are my beloved Son; with you I am well pleased'" (3:21–22).

Jesus was unashamed to identify with us, so let's be unashamed to identify with him.

Changing Our Story with God's Story

Water baptism changes our life by pointing to three greater baptisms. It points us to salvation and sanctification via *Spirit baptism*. It warns us of incineration by *fire baptism*. And it encourages through *Christ's identification with us in his baptism*.

Summary: What does water baptism do? *Use baptism to seek salvation, flee incineration, and enjoy identification with Jesus.*

Question: How will Jesus's identifying with sinners help you not identify with sin today?

Prayer: Blessed Baptizer, please perform what baptism pictures. Wash me, protect me, and identify with me for your glory and my good.

God's painful plan is always better than the devil's easy plan.

Hear
God's Story

Change
Your Story

Tell
the Story

Change
Others' Stories

10

Toughened by Temptation

LUKE 4:1-15

How often have you thought, "I must not be a Christian if I'm tempted like this"? A sinful idea or image comes into our minds, and we ask ourselves, "How can I think that or want that and still be a Christian? Why does God allow me to be tempted like this?" Or to put it simply, *What's the point of temptation?* In Luke 4:1–15, we read about three painful temptations of Jesus and discover three ways God uses temptation for our good.

Temptation Tests Our Faith in God's Provision 4:1-4

Famished after forty days of fasting in the wilderness, Jesus heard the devil sneering: "If you are the Son of God, command this stone to become bread" (4:3). Satan essentially was saying, "The Son of God, hungry? How ridiculous. Does God really care for you? Take matters into your own hands and provide for yourself" (4:3).

God promised his Son, just as he promises all his children, that he would provide for his needs if he would trust him. The devil tempted Jesus to doubt God's provision and instead rely on his own provision.

Did Jesus succumb? Never! Jesus answered the devil, "It is written, 'Man shall not live by bread alone'" (4:4). Some things are more important than eating, even when we're starving. Jesus would not sacrifice his trust in God to satisfy his hunger. His faith in God's provision was strengthened by passing this test.

Trusting God is more important than eating food, even when we're starving.

I trust God's daily provision, but I'm tempted to doubt God's overall plan.

Temptation Tests Our Faith in God's Plan 4:5–8

At Jesus's weakest point, the devil offered Jesus world power for one bow. "To you I will give all this authority and their glory, for it has been delivered to me, and I give it to whom I will. If you, then, will worship me, it will all be yours" (4:5–7). What an offer! The whole world for one second of devil worship.

Whose plan will Jesus follow? God's plan of suffering for years, then the crown? Or the Devil's plan of a second of worship, then the crown? "Jesus answered him, 'It is written, "You shall worship the Lord your God, and him only shall you serve"'" (4:8). His faith in God's plan was strengthened by this test.

God's painful plan is always better than the devil's easy plan.

What if God's plan involves danger?

Temptation Tests Our Faith in God's Protection 4:9–12

The devil next took Jesus to the pinnacle of the temple and taunted him into jumping off and trusting God to look after him:

> If you are the Son of God, throw yourself down from here, for it is written,
>
> > "He will command his angels concerning you,
> >   to guard you,"
> and
>
> > "On their hands they will bear you up,
> >   lest you strike your foot against a stone." (4:9–11)

Satan is saying, "So, you say you believe in God. Let's see how much you really believe. You've been quoting Scripture to me; let's see how much you trust this verse. You say God cares for you; let's see how precious you are to God."

Jesus could easily have done this, but he would have done it for the wrong reason. It's one thing to trust God's protection from evil, but another to trust God's protection when doing evil. That's why Jesus answered him, "It is said, 'You shall not put the Lord your God to the test'" (4:12). His faith in God's protection was strengthened by this test.

God tests us; we don't test God.

Changing Our Story with God's Story

Temptation tests our faith to strengthen it. Look at how Jesus was strengthened through his terrible temptations. After his time in the wilderness, Jesus returned in the power of the Spirit to Galilee, and a report about him went out through all the surrounding country. He taught in their synagogues, being glorified by all (4:13–15). Jesus uses his Story of testing to change our story of testing (Heb. 4:15).

Summary: What's the point in temptation? *Follow Jesus in using the test of temptation to strengthen your faith in God's provision, plan, and protection.*

Question: Which temptation is strengthening your faith today?

Prayer: Holy Jesus, you were tempted more than me and more than anyone ever. But you passed the test and can encourage me in my tests so that I too come out of it stronger rather than weaker, with a better story rather than a worse one.

God shows favor not favoritism.

11

What Is the Gospel?

LUKE 4:16–30

"What is the gospel?" That's such a simple question, yet it's frighteningly easy to get wrong. We'd expect unbelievers to get it wrong—and they do, usually answering with various versions of "Try your best. Be nice. Do good." That's not the gospel. But believers get it wrong too, with answers that also tend to emphasize the human response to the gospel. "Believe, repent, seek, call, etc." That's not the gospel either, as is clear to any who try to find joy in their faith, repentance, and so on.

So, *what is the gospel?* Who better than Jesus to give us the answer, which he did in Luke 4:16–30, when he preached his first sermon in his home synagogue in Nazareth.

The Gospel Is a Proclamation of Good News 4:16–18

Jesus loved his local church, and he loved to read the Bible there. One day he was given the scroll of Isaiah. He unrolled it to chapter 61, and began to read:

> The Spirit of the Lord is upon me,
>   because he has anointed me
>   to proclaim good news to the poor. (4:18)

Jesus's first job was to issue a royal proclamation. This was no ordinary announcement that disappeared into the ether. A proclamation produced what it proclaimed. In this case, the proclaimer proclaimed a proclamation of good news for the poor. Although most kings didn't bother with the poor, this merciful King made them his first priority. He came into their sad world with good news, into their poor world with spiritual riches.

The gospel is true news in a fake news world.

But I'm not poor. Is the gospel also for me?

The Gospel Is a Proclamation of Freedom 4:18

Jesus then turns to those enslaved by prison walls, cruel masters, dreadful disabilities, and oppressive mental illness. "He has sent me to proclaim liberty to the captives and recovering of sight to the blind, to set at liberty those who are oppressed" (4:18). *Freedom!* What a rare word for prisoners, the disabled, and the mentally ill. All they had known was limitation, incarceration, captivity, confinement, and bondage. But here's someone who comes along and proclaims: *Freedom! Liberation! Emancipation! Release!* Chains fall off, walls crumble, and bars break.

Sin promises freedom, but the gospel proclaims freedom.

What do I do to get this freedom?

The Gospel Is a Proclamation of Grace 4:19

The third part of this proclamation is "to proclaim the year of the Lord's favor" (4:19). In Leviticus 25, God proclaimed every fiftieth year as the Year of Jubilee. All debts were to be forgiven, all slaves and prisoners were to be freed, all forfeited property was to be returned to the original owners, and everyone was to rest from work. This was the year of the Lord's favor, a year in which Israel was to celebrate the grace of God.

Imagine you were poor, a slave, a prisoner, or a debtor in Israel. It's one second to midnight on the last day of the forty-ninth year. One second later the horn blows, and you're free! What powerful pity! What great grace!

God shows favor not favoritism.

Changing Our Story with God's Story

You don't need to wait until the fiftieth year for the year of the Lord's favor. Every time the gospel is preached, the Jubilee horn is blown. Do you hear it? How does it make you feel? Has it blown all the way into your heart, bringing riches, freedom, and grace? It's a proclamation of "Done!" not a demand to "Do!"

Summary: What is the gospel? *Receive God's Jubilee proclamation of good news, freedom, and grace.*

Question: How will this gospel message help you to proclaim the gospel today?

Prayer: Liberator, thank you for securing my freedom and releasing my joy. Your Jubilee is my jubilation. Help me to proclaim your Jubilee to others so that they may rejoice in your grace too.

With Jesus we won't just be fishing, we'll be catching.

Hear
God's Story

Change
Your Story

Tell
the Story

Change
Others' Stories

12

My Best Fishing Tip

LUKE 5:1-11

An eighty-year-old women gave me the best-ever fishing tip, and I want to share it with you. Her tip has proven to be better than anything I've learned from the Outdoor Channel. Perhaps on my next fishing trip I'll have as much success as the discouraged disciples in Luke 5:1-11. This passage also gives an encouraging answer to the question, *"What should I do when I'm discouraged about my soul fishing?"*

Jesus Catches Souls 5:1-3

Crowds of people were listening to Jesus teach the word of God beside the lake of Gennesaret. The audience was so big and so eager that "they were pressing in on [Jesus] to hear the word of God" (5:1). In danger of being mobbed and pushed into the lake, Jesus spotted Simon's boat, got in, pushed out a little, sat down, and taught the people from the boat (5:2-3). What an inspiring and encouraging sight! Wouldn't you love to have seen that? Jesus was catching multiple souls with the word of God. His teaching drew multitudes to press into the kingdom.

Jesus's words are the best bait.

Jesus is a master teacher, but I'm not Jesus.

Jesus Catches Fish 5:4–10

"When [Jesus] had finished speaking, he said to Simon, 'Put out into the deep and let down your nets for a catch' And Simon answered, 'Master, we toiled all night and took nothing! But at your word I will let down the nets'" (5:4–5).

It was the worst time for fishing (daytime), it was the worst place for fishing (deep waters), and they had the worst attitude for fishing (pessimism). But, despite so much against them, one thing was for them: Jesus's word. "At your word I will let down the nets" (5:5). Jesus's word can overpower nature and human nature. And it did. They caught so many fish, they had to ask another boat to help, and both were so heavy with fish they were beginning to sink (5:6–7).

The best angler is better than the worst conditions.

So, what's the big lesson here?

Jesus's Students Will Catch People 5:8–11

The disciples were astonished at the catch. "When Simon Peter saw it, he fell down at Jesus' knees, saying, 'Depart from me, for I am a sinful man, O Lord'" (5:8). He knew this was not natural but supernatural, this was not his fishing skill but Christ's divine power. Jesus comforted Simon with the biggest words in this passage: "Do not be afraid; from now on you will be catching men" (5:10). This was the point of the miracle. Jesus was saying, "You've seen me catch lots of people and lots of fish. Now leave your fishing, follow me, and you'll catch lots of people too." What did they do? "And when they had brought their boats to land, they left everything and followed him" (5:11).

With Jesus we won't just be fishing, we'll be catching.

Changing Our Story with God's Story

You're still waiting for that fishing tip, aren't you? Lean in, and I'll whisper it to you. As a seminary student, I interned at an inner-city church in Glasgow. At the first midweek prayer meeting, I preached on this passage. Afterward, a frail eighty-year-old Christian woman came up to me with a lovely smile on her face and repeated my text to me: "Launch out into the deep!" (5:4 KJV).

At the end of every church meeting for the rest of the summer, she would say the same thing: "Launch out into the deep!" I think she sensed my pessimism and discouragement about the church's mission in that destitute area, and wanted to both challenge and encourage me to keep fishing in unpromising waters. With her weekly words, I did, and although my net didn't break, I know at least one fish was caught. An eighty-year-old woman gave me the best fishing tip of my life.

Summary: What should I do when I'm discouraged by my lack of fish? *Learn skill, courage, and faith from the master angler to increase your catch.*

Question: What do you need to make you a better soul-angler: skill, courage, or faith?

Prayer: Master Angler, give me the skill, courage, and faith I need to catch souls for you.

Jesus wants us feasting more than fasting.

Hear
God's Story

Change
Your Story

Tell
the Story

Change
Others' Stories

13

Feasting or Fasting?

LUKE 5:27–39

What's more Christian: feasting or fasting? Both are Christian, but which is more Christian? *Which is more characteristic of the Christian era: festive celebration or funeral lamentation? Which does your character lean toward: feasting or fasting?* Luke 5:27–39 helps us discover whether we are to be feasters or fasters.

Jesus Feasts with Sinners 5:27-32

When Jesus called Levi the tax collector to follow him, Levi left his job, followed him, prepared a great feast in his house, and invited lots of other tax collectors to eat and drink with him and Jesus (5:27–29). What an amazing sight! The Son of God feasting with the lowest ranked people and the highest ranked sinners. How happy everyone must have been!

Not quite: "The Pharisees and their scribes grumbled at his disciples, saying, 'Why do you eat and drink with tax collectors and sinners?'" (5:30). Their attempt to shame Jesus and his disciples backfired badly. Instead of being embarrassed about his new friends and distancing himself from them, Jesus owned them and even expressed his preference for them. "Those who are well," he explained, "have no need of a physician, but those who are sick. I have not come to call the righteous but sinners to repentance" (5:31–32).

Jesus did not deny that his dinner companions were the worst sinners, but rather delighted in them. This was not a contradiction of his mission, but an expression of it. The sicker the sinners, the better, as far as Jesus was concerned. He didn't come to fast with the healthiest but to feast with the sickest. The Pharisees tried to spoil the party, but Jesus enlivened it. Notice, also, he didn't just eat with sinners; he healed them by calling them to repentance.

Jesus socialized with sinners but didn't socialize their sin.

Jesus enjoys feasting with sinners,
but can sinners enjoy feasting with Jesus?

Sinners Feast with Jesus 5:33–39

Surely now the Pharisees would realize that they weren't going to trip Jesus up on anything to do with feasting or fasting. But, despite having struck out already, they tried again. This time, they complained that although John's disciples would fast, Jesus's disciples ate and drank (5:33). This was another attempt to throw a wet blanket on Jesus's gospel party by spoiling the disciples' joy in Jesus.

Jesus was having none of it. He said to them, "Can you make wedding guests fast while the bridegroom is with them?" (5:34). He was saying, "I've come to a wedding not a funeral. Sure, there's a funeral ahead (5:35), but until then, we're going to have a party. We're going to celebrate my wedding to my bride."

He used two other pictures to justify his festival spirit: "I haven't come to patch up a worn-out religion; I've come with a whole new piece of cloth. And I haven't come to waste my wine by putting it in old wineskins. Instead, I'm all about new wine in new wineskins so that the maximum number can drink and gladden their hearts" (see 5:36–39). Whether it's a restaurant, a wedding, or a vineyard, we're here to feast not fast.

Jesus wants us feasting more than fasting.

Changing Our Story with God's Story

Jesus does not deny the place of fasting. But in the gospel era, it has a relatively minor place compared to the place of feasting. The Christian is to be primarily characterized by the festal joy Jesus has given us. Yes, there will be some seasons of sadness, but Christ has given us more reasons for gladness.

Summary: Which is more characteristic of the Christian era: festive celebration or funeral lamentation? *Jesus calls sinners to festive celebration through gospel healing and gospel marriage.*

Question: How will you enjoy joy from gospel healing and gospel marriage today?

Prayer: Lord Jesus, thank you for inviting me to your gospel dinner party. Help me to eat and drink in your joy, and show it to all, no matter how strongly religious people may object.

Jesus has empathetic authority and authoritative empathy.

Hear
God's Story

Change
Your Story

Tell
the Story

Change
Others' Stories

14

A Better Guide Than Oprah

LUKE 7:1–17

Who's your favorite boss? Your favorite coach? Your favorite teacher? Your favorite mentor? What do they all have in common? They all have a combination of authority and empathy, don't they? Researchers have found that we will not let anyone be our guide unless they have both authority and empathy. We want guides we can both respect for their competence and trust for their compassion.

If that's true in work, sports, and school, how much more when it comes to our souls? Who has so much authority and empathy that we can trust him to be the guide of our souls? Luke 7:1–17 points us to a spiritual guide with full authority and perfect empathy.

Jesus Is an Authoritative Guide 7:1–10

Authority is the result of competence. We need to know that our guide knows what he's doing. Does Jesus know what he's doing, and does he have lots of experience in doing it? Let's ask a Roman centurion.

The centurion's best servant was dying and, for all his power and authority, there was nothing this general could do about it (7:2). But when "the centurion heard about [Jesus], he sent to him elders of the Jews, asking him to come and heal his servant" (7:3). Jesus agreed, but as he approached the house, "the centurion sent friends, saying to him, 'Lord, do not trouble yourself, for I am not worthy to have you come under my roof. Therefore I did not presume to come to you. But say the word, and let my servant be healed. For I too am a man set under authority, with soldiers under me: and I say to one, "Go," and he goes; and to another, "Come," and he comes; and to my servant, "Do this," and he does it'" (7:6–8).

This powerful, authoritative centurion recognized that Jesus had even more powerful authority than he had and could simply command healing from a distance. Jesus was stunned and said, "'I tell you, not even in Israel have I found such faith.' And when those who had been sent returned to the house, they found the servant well" (7:9–10). Now that's authority we can respect.

Ability authors authority.

Jesus has authority, but does he have empathy?

Jesus Is an Empathetic Guide 7:11–17

Oprah Winfrey, a popular guide for millions, once said that the three things every human being wants most are to be seen, heard, and understood. That's the heart of empathy, and Jesus had it in spades, as this next story demonstrates.

Jesus saw a dead man being carried out of the town for burial, the only son of a widow (7:12). "When the Lord saw her, he had compassion on her and said to her, 'Do not weep'" (7:13). Jesus was saying, "I see you, I hear you, I understand you." But not only did he have far more empathy than Oprah, he had far more power. He touched the stretcher and said, "'Young man, I say to you, arise.' And the dead man sat up and began to speak, and Jesus gave him to his mother" (7:14–15).

Jesus has empathetic authority and authoritative empathy.

Changing Our Story with God's Story

Do you want a spiritual guide you can respect and trust? Use Christ's authority to build respect for him, and Christ's empathy to build trust in him. If you do, you'll join the people of Jesus's day who "glorified God, saying, 'A great prophet has arisen among us!' and 'God has visited his people!' And this report about him spread through the whole of Judea and all the surrounding country" (7:16–17). When Christ is the guide of our story, we want others to have his guidance too.

Summary: Who has so much authority and empathy that we can trust him to be the guide of our souls? *Use Christ's authority to build respect for his guidance, and Christ's empathy to build trust in his guidance.*

Question: Whose story can you change today by being an authoritative and empathetic guide like Christ?

Prayer: My Guide, I praise you for your authoritative empathy and empathetic authority. Help me to respect and trust your guidance.

Fertilize your love for Christ by realizing your forgiveness by Christ.

Hear
God's Story

Change
Your Story

Tell
the Story

Change
Others' Stories

15

A Love Fertilizer

LUKE 7:36–50

How do I love Christ more? Christ is so lovable, and worthy of so much love, and yet I do not love him as he deserves. I do not love him as I want to love him. True, I love him more than I did when I was an unbeliever. But it's still sapling love. I want cedar love. I want sequoia redwood love. *How do I grow my sapling love into redwood love?* Jesus gives us two big bags of love fertilizer in Luke 7:36–50.

Big Debt Forgiveness Grows Big Love 7:36–43

This is one of only two occasions in the Bible when any Pharisee showed any kindness to Christ. But, as we'll see, although Simon had an open and hospitable home, he had a closed and inhospitable heart.

While Jesus was reclining at Simon the Pharisee's supper table, a stunning scene unfolded. "Behold, a woman of the city, who was a sinner, when she learned that he was reclining at table in the Pharisee's house, brought an alabaster flask of ointment, and standing behind him at his feet, weeping, she began to wet his feet with her tears and wiped them with the hair of her head and kissed his feet and anointed them with the ointment" (7:37–38).

Simon the Pharisee was appalled, and said to himself, "If this man were a prophet, he would have known who and what sort of woman this is who is touching him, for she is a sinner" (7:39). Imagine, a holy man letting such an unholy woman touch him. Disgusting!

Sensing Simon's horror, Jesus told him a parable in which a lender cancelled the debts of two men, one a big debt and the other a small debt. "Now which of them will love him more?" Jesus asked (7:42). Simon couldn't do grace, but he could do math, and answered rightly, if a little reluctantly, "The one, I suppose, for whom he cancelled the larger debt" (7:43).

The greater the cancellation, the greater the celebration.

Debt cancellation would help me love my bank. But how does it help me love Christ?

Big Sin Forgiveness Grows Big Love 7:44–50

Having given Simon some math practice, Jesus gave Simon some grace practice. Jesus essentially said, "This woman washed my feet with her tears, wiped them with her hair, kissed them with her lips, and anointed my head with oil. What did you do? Nothing!" (7:44–46). Why? Why such a difference?

"Her sins, which are many, are forgiven—for she loved much. But he who is forgiven little, loves little" (7:47). Her greater forgiveness resulted in greater love. In contrast, Simon's little love revealed little forgiveness.

Jesus was not saying that the woman needed more forgiveness than Simon. Nor was Jesus saying that Simon's lack of love was understandable because he hadn't sinned as much as her. He was saying, "Simon, if you knew how sinful you are, and if you knew how much forgiveness you need, you wouldn't find your heart so cold toward me and hostile toward sinners."

Fertilize your love for Christ by realizing your forgiveness by Christ.

Changing Our Story with God's Story

So, should I sin more so I can be forgiven more, so I can love Jesus more? That's like saying, "Should I pour poison on my garden so that I can grow better vegetables?" No, we don't need more sin to get more forgiveness. We need a greater appreciation of forgiveness to get a greater experience of love. We need to realize forgiveness more, measure it more, savor it more. The forgiveness of past sin is a fertilizer for present love. Forgiven sin is love fertilizer but future sin is love poisoner.

Summary: How do I grow my sapling love into redwood love? *Fertilize your love by realizing, measuring, and savoring your forgiveness.*

Question: Which forgiven sin will you fertilize your love with today?

Prayer: Sin-Canceler and Love-Fertilizer, fertilize my love by helping me to weigh, count, and measure your forgiveness. Amen.

A big second place for Christ is still not first place for Christ.

16

Me First!

LUKE 9:57–62

Many want to follow Christ . . . second. Me first, Christ second. Of course, we never put it that way. We still call him "Lord." We still *say* he's first, but our lives and choices say he's second. And if he's second, he's not Lord. As someone said, "Christ is Lord of all, or he is not Lord at all."

How do we put Christ second, and how can we put him first? Luke 9:57–62 records three interactions between Jesus and three potential disciples that spotlight three rival lords to Jesus.

We Put Comfort First 9:57–58

"As they were going along the road, someone said to him, 'I will follow you wherever you go'" (9:57). Jesus challenged the reality of this offer and promise, saying, "Foxes have holes, and birds of the air have nests, but the Son of Man has nowhere to lay his head" (9:58). Knowing that personal comfort was this man's real lord, Jesus told him that following him meant living worse than animals. You won't have a foxhole or even a bird's nest to sleep in. Comfort first or Christ first?

A big second place for Christ is still not first place for Christ.

Personal comfort isn't a big deal to me.
What else can slip into first place?

We Put Family First 9:59–60

"Me first! Me first!" We expect to hear that from children playing games in the yard. We don't expect to hear it from potential disciples of Christ. Yet here we do.

"Me first!" was implicit in the first interaction, but it's explicit in the second and third. When Jesus called the second man to follow him, he replied "Lord, let me first go and bury my father" (9:59).

What a contradiction. He starts with "Lord," then says "me first." "Lord . . . me first." He says Jesus is Lord of his life, but then he lets it slip that he's really the lord of his life. Which is why Jesus said, "Leave the dead to bury their own dead. But as for you, go and proclaim the kingdom of God" (9:60). Expanding the Lord's family must take priority over burying one's own family.

Giving life with the gospel is more important than burying the dead with a spade.

I'm going to follow Christ soon, just as soon as I'm not so busy.

We Put Work First 9:61–62

"Yet another said, 'I will follow you, Lord, but let me first say farewell to those at my home'" (9:61). Did you notice it? Another "Lord . . . me first."

Like the second man, this man seems to put saying farewell to his family before following Christ. But Jesus's answer reveals that the man was really putting his job first. "Jesus said to him, 'No one who puts his hand to the plow and looks back is fit for the kingdom of God'" (9:62). A farmer who plows while looking backward is not going to be a farmer for long. Jesus is basically giving the man a choice: plowing or preaching? Dollars or discipleship?

When we're looking back, we're not looking to Christ.

Changing Our Story with God's Story

When I was converted in my early twenties, I decided to leave my job in financial services. I loved business, but my job involved too many moral compromises. I was sensing God's call to the ministry, but instead I decided, "I'll start my own business and give the money to the Lord." Despite the spiritual language, I was putting business first, not Christ. So Christ took it all away. My business failed, and I lost all my money. Use my story and this story to identify rival lords, and to ensure that Christ is Lord of all on every page of our story.

Summary: How do we put Christ second, and how can we put him first? *When tempted to put comfort, family, or work first, remember that Christ is Lord of all, or he is not Lord at all.*

Question: In which area of life are you shouting "Lord!" but whispering "me first."

Prayer: Lord of All, help me never to say "me first" but always "Jesus first" so that I can be your wholehearted follower.

My great joy is souls being saved, but my greatest joy is my soul being saved.

17

Rejection and Rejoicing

LUKE 10:1–24

The fear of rejection can stop the fun of rejoicing. When I was in my late teens and early twenties, I was terrified of romantic rejection. I was so scared of hearing young women say no if I were to ask them for a date that I didn't bother to even ask (my wife Shona is pretty happy about that). This practice helped me to avoid rejection, but it also voided the potential joy of hearing a yes.

For many of us, the fear of gospel rejection prevents the fun of gospel rejoicing. We're so afraid of people saying no to the gospel that we don't even give them the chance to say yes. In doing so, we not only damn them but we dam up the huge reservoir of potential joy in seeing people come to faith. *How can we overcome the fear of gospel rejection?* Jesus helped his disciples do this in Luke 10:1–24.

We Will Be Rejected 10:1–16

Jesus sent out seventy-two disciples ahead of him to preach and pray (10:1). He held out the prospect of a bountiful harvest of souls but, seeing the obstacle of limited laborers, called them to pray for more (10:2). So far, so optimistic.

But then his tone changes. "I am sending you out as lambs in the midst of wolves" (10:3). Some will accept your offer of peace, whereas others will throw it back in your faces (10:6). Some will receive you (10:7–8), others will reject you (10:10). When whole towns repudiate you, don't wallow in self-pity. Because "the one who rejects you rejects me, and the one who rejects me rejects him who sent me" (10:16). It's not you; it's me. It's not even me; it's God. Jesus felt that rejection deeply and painfully.

Gospel rejection is God rejection.

But I still don't know if the pain of rejection is worth it.

We Will Rejoice 10:17–20

The disciples went out in fear but they "returned with joy, saying, 'Lord, even the demons are subject to us in your name!'" (10:17). They reveled together in the power of the gospel to defeat Satan and all his minions (10:18–19).

But Jesus pointed them to an even greater joy that did not depend on the success of the gospel: "Do not rejoice in this, that the spirits are subject to you, but rejoice that your names are written in heaven" (10:20). Jesus joined them in celebrating the salvation of others, but wanted their primary joy to be their own salvation.

My great joy is souls being saved, but my greatest joy is my soul being saved.

Is my personal joy a legitimate outreach motivation? Yes, because Jesus used it too.

Jesus Will Rejoice 10:21–24

When Jesus saw the disciples' gospel success, he rejoiced in it with them. It's the only time in the Gospels that we read explicitly of Jesus's joy. He delighted especially in his Father's sovereign salvation of children and the childlike, even if the wise and understanding didn't get it. Inspired by the Holy Spirit, he delighted in his Father graciously opening people's eyes to see who he and the Father really were (10:21–22). It was a new era of gospel blessing, expansion, and rejoicing (10:23).

Gospel success is God's success.

Changing Our Story with God's Story

How many times have we allowed the fear of gospel rejection to damn souls and dam up gospel rejoicing? How many times have we allowed that phobia to damn souls and dam up gospel rejoicing on earth and in heaven, in our hearts and in the heart of Christ? Instead, let's swim in the lake of gospel rejoicing and from there bring gospel water to parched souls, even if they pour it out on the sand of unbelief.

Summary: How can we overcome the fear of gospel rejection? *Use the potential of gospel rejoicing to overcome the potential pain of gospel rejection.*

Question: How can you use the potential joy of gospel success to overcome your present fear of gospel rejection?

Prayer: Happy God, use the happiness of my salvation, and others' salvation, to fuel happy evangelism and overcome gospel rejection.

If we try to do and
live, we'll not do—
and we will die.

18

Do and Die

LUKE 10:25–37

What is the biggest spiritual problem in the world today? It's exactly the same as the biggest problem in Bible times. Doing good. Or, more precisely, doing good for salvation. It's the biggest spiritual problem because doing good cannot be done. It's not just that we cannot do enough good; we simply cannot do any good (Rom. 3:12). But that doesn't stop most from trying. *How do we solve the massive problem that doing does nothing?* Jesus has a surprising answer for us in Luke 10:25–37.

Do and Live 10:25–28

If someone asked you, "How can I be saved?" would you ever answer, "Turn to the Ten Commandments"? That's what Jesus did when a lawyer asked him, "What shall I do to inherit eternal life?" (10:25). Jesus's response? "What is written in the Law? How do you read it?" (10:26). Jesus pointed him to the law not the gospel, to Exodus 20 not John 3:16.

The lawyer knew the law very well and answered, "You shall love the Lord your God with all your heart and with all your soul and with all your strength and with all your mind, and your neighbor as yourself" (10:27). You can almost see his smug expression, can't you? "How easy is this!"

Jesus gave him full marks. "You have answered correctly" (10:28). Now we're expecting the gospel, aren't we? But instead of "believe and live," Jesus says, "Do this, and you will live."

If we do, we will live.

Wait . . . what? Has Jesus forgotten the gospel?

Do and Die 10:29–37

Jesus got another chance to get the gospel right when the lawyer, "desiring to justify himself, said to Jesus, 'And who is my neighbor?'" (10:29). There's a little clue there that Jesus's unconventional approach was actually getting through to the lawyer's heart. Did you notice it? His question, "Who is my neighbor?" was motivated by his desire to justify himself. Though he recited the law perfectly, he knew he'd never kept it perfectly. He therefore shifted from prosecution mode to defense mode. Jesus got to his heart, and it hurt.

So, now Jesus gives him the gospel, right? Nope, he gives him even more law through the parable of the good Samaritan, who cared for a dying man when a priest and Levite left him for dead (10:30–35). Jesus asked, "Which of these three, do you think, proved to be a neighbor to the man who fell among the robbers?" (10:36). "The one who showed him mercy," replied the lawyer.

His defense was going pretty well up to this point. But then came the dagger thrust. Jesus said to him, "You go, and do likewise." What? He did it again. Jesus missed the gospel. "Go and do" instead of "come and rest." What's going on?

Jesus knew he'd already pierced the lawyer's heart with the law. Now he thrusts it deep into his heart to kill him (spiritually). He knew that "go and do" would result in "go and die." As the lawyer tried to love like the good Samaritan, he would realize he was a bad Israelite. The good Samaritan story would murder his self-sufficiency, self-righteousness, self-confidence, and self-love. He was about to experience a slow death by doing, which would prepare him for immediate life by believing. Christ compassionately convicts.

If we try to do and live, we'll not do—and we will die.

Changing Our Story with God's Story

The law says, "Do and live." The gospel says, "Live, and you'll do." Like the victim in this parable, we are dying and helpless sinners. But Jesus comes along as *the* good Samaritan to give us life and help. He gives what we do not have; he does what we cannot do; he is what we'll never be.

Summary: How do we solve the massive problem that doing does nothing? *Do more and more until you die enough to believe.*

Question: Who will you "kill" today with God's law so that they seek life in God's love?

Prayer: Good Samaritan, give me life through faith so that I can live by faith. Amen.

A wrong perspective results in wrong priorities.

19

How Do I Decrease Stress and Increase Spirituality?

LUKE 10:38–42

Stress sickens the soul. Yes, stress causes bodily disease (some estimate that 90 percent of doctor visits are stress related), but it also causes soul disease. Stress and spirituality are mortal enemies. *How do I decrease stress and increase spirituality?*

The problem existed in Jesus's day too and in Luke 10:38–42 Jesus diagnosed the problem and issued the prescription.

Jesus Discourages the Stressed Life

Mary, Martha, and Lazarus were Jesus's best friends, aside from his twelve disciples. They lived in Bethany, a suburb of Jerusalem, and Jesus often dropped in on them to be refreshed by their friendship, fellowship, and hospitality.

When Jesus knocked on the door one day, Martha ran to the kitchen and started fixing a meal for her surprise guest, while Mary sat down at Jesus's feet to listen to his teaching (10:38–39).

This was really bugging Martha, who was "distracted with much serving" (10:40). She's slaving in the kitchen while her sister's lounging in the living room. Eventually she lost it, burst into the room, marched up to Jesus, and protested, "Lord, do you not care that my sister has left me to serve alone? Tell her then to help me" (10:40).

Here we have two very different sisters representing two very different ways of living. Mary was preoccupied with Jesus, Martha with herself. Mary saw an opportunity to learn; Martha saw meat and potatoes. Mary was centered on Christ; Martha was distracted from Christ. Mary needed the Lord's care; Martha felt he didn't care.

How did Jesus respond? First, he addresses her affectionately: "Martha, Martha." It's a term of endearment like "My dear, dear Martha." Second, he acknowledges her turmoil: "You are anxious and troubled about many things." Third, he calls her away from many optional things to the one necessary thing (himself): "One thing is necessary." He's saying, "Your company means more to me than your cooking. You've become so distracted with serving that you've forgotten the one you're trying to serve" (10:41–42).

A wrong perspective results in wrong priorities.

If stress is the problem, what's the solution?

Jesus Encourages the Spiritual Life

Jesus pointed to Mary as an example to follow: "Mary has chosen the good portion, which will not be taken away from her" (10:42).

Sitting at a teacher's feet was like saying, "I am a disciple, a student, of this teacher." It indicated submission and teachability. Mary appears three times in the Gospels, and each time she is at the feet of Jesus. Here, she listens to his word (Luke 10:39). When Lazarus dies, she falls at his feet and pours out her heart (John 11:32). And she pours out perfume and worship on his feet (John 12:3). Mary sits while Martha stresses.

"Mary has chosen the good portion, which will not be taken away from her." Martha focused on food that would be forgotten, but Mary focused on eternal food that would benefit her forever. Martha was making lots of starters, but Mary had chosen the steak. Martha was preparing a banquet, while Mary was having one.

Jesus essentially said, "Martha, copy your sister. Put down your rolling pin and apron and sit at my feet. Enjoy me, and let me enjoy you. Leave all the other stuff undone and have a calm conversation with me. Unrushed. Unhurried. Let's sit down and catch up." In the previous verses, Jesus had preached the law to the lawyer. "Go and do." Here he preaches the gospel to Martha, "Come and sit." So kind, so tender.

Spiritual life sprouts by sitting down.

Changing Our Story with God's Story

Jesus would rather feed us than be fed by us. He'd rather serve us than be served by us. He prizes our friendship and our fellowship more than all our service. As Warren Wiersbe said, "Few things are as damaging to the Christian life as trying to work for Christ without taking time to commune with Christ."[1]

Summary: How do I decrease stress and increase spirituality? *Spend time learning and loving at the feet of Jesus.*

Question: How can you spend more time at Christ's feet and less time in the devil's kitchen?

Prayer: Soul-Calmer, when I'm stressed on my feet, help me to find rest at your feet.

1 Warren W. Wiersbe, *Be Compassionate (Luke 1-13): Let the World Know That Jesus Cares* (Colorado Springs: David C. Cook, 2010), 140.

God's door opens to confident thudding not nervous tapping.

20

Three Solutions to Prayer Problems

LUKE 11:5-13

"I'm really good at praying," said no Christian ever. We know we should pray. We start praying. But soon we give up. Or we pray with no expectation of an answer. Or we pray for the wrong things. Prayer becomes a problem rather than a solution, and it depresses us rather than encourages us. *How can we pray in a way that solves our problems rather than adds to them?* Jesus guides us to that happy place in Luke 11:5-13.

The disciples had the same issues with prayer as we do, and one day asked Jesus, "Teach us to pray" (Luke 11:1). Jesus sympathized with them, started his prayer class with the model of the Lord's Prayer (11:2-4), then addressed three problems with prayer (11:5-13).

Persistent Prayer Will Be Answered Prayer 11:5-8

It's midnight, a hungry friend arrives at your door, you have no food, and there's no Walmart for miles. What do you do? The man in our story decided to bang on his neighbor's door until he annoyed him enough to leave his bed to give him bread (11:5-8).

The man's appeal to friendship and hunger failed. But his persistent pleading succeeded. He simply wouldn't give up. More than that, he was impudent in his persistence. He wasn't just tapping the door every few minutes; he was banging it nonstop. Eventually this friend was so irked that he got up and gave the man what he needed, just to make him go away. (Parents know what this feels like.)

When we give up prayer, we give up more than prayer.

I keep on praying, but I'm doubtful it works.

Confident Prayer Will Be Answered Prayer 11:9–10

"I know you probably won't help me with this, but I suppose I should ask you anyway." How would you feel if someone said that to you? I would say something like, "You're right, I'm not helping you with that." The half-hearted lack of confidence is insulting.

But if someone said, "I'm asking you for help because I know you love to help people," that would open your heart, wouldn't it? That's the kind of God-confidence Jesus is encouraging when he says, "And I tell you, ask, and it will be given to you; seek, and you will find; knock, and it will be opened to you. For everyone who asks receives, and the one who seeks finds, and to the one who knocks it will be opened" (11:9–10).

God's door opens to confident thudding not nervous tapping.

So, if I ask for a red Corvette, I'll get one?

Spiritual Prayer Will Be Answered Prayer 11:11–13

Would you ever ask your dad for a snake or a scorpion? Then why ask God for a Corvette? Instead, Jesus says, ask for the Holy Spirit because your heavenly Father loves to give the best of gifts to his children. "What father among you, if his son asks for a fish, will instead of a fish give him a serpent; or if he asks for an egg, will give him a scorpion? If you then, who are evil, know how to give good gifts to your children, how much more will the heavenly Father give the Holy Spirit to those who ask him!" (11:11–13). God may give us a red Corvette, but we shouldn't pray for one.

Why ask for a Corvette, when you can have Christ?

Changing Our Story with God's Story

This story tells us the kind of story God wants for all of us. He wants us to have a prayer life that's characterized by persistent, confident, spiritual prayers.

Summary: How can we pray in a way that solves our problems rather than adds to them? *Pray persistently, confidently, and spiritually for the greatest answers to prayer.*

Question: How can you increase persistence, confidence, and spirituality in your prayers?

Prayer: Giving God, help me to pray for your best gifts with persistence, confidence, and spirituality. Amen.

If I make life about money, money will take my life.

 Hear
God's Story

Change
Your Story

Tell
the Story

Change
Others' Stories

21

Money, Money, Money

LUKE 12:13-21

Life is money and money is life. That's the essence of a recent report which found that "money dominates our daily thoughts. . . . About one in four Americans said that money is the thing they think about most on a daily basis — and another one in four spent most of their time thinking about work" (which is closely related to money).[1]

What about the other 50 percent? Half are seniors whose main priority has moved from wealth to health, and the others are young people who are pursuing marriage, which usually accelerates the pursuit of money!

What happens when money is life and life is money? In Luke 12:13–21, Jesus warns of two serious consequences.

Greed Divides 12:13-15

One day someone with a money problem came to Jesus. He was in a dispute with his brother over an inheritance and wanted Jesus's help to get his proper share. Jesus refused to get involved: "Man, who made me a judge or arbitrator over you?" (12:14). In other words, "Money is not my mission, man!" Money makes people fight one another; Jesus came to make people love one another. Money kills, but Jesus gives life. Money disputes cause many deaths.

---

1 Mark Fahey and Nicholas Wells, "Americans Think about Money and Work More Than Sex, Survey Finds," NBCNews.com, September 9, 2015, https://www.nbcnews .com/.

Out of deep concern for their souls, Jesus issued a general warning: "Take care, and be on your guard against all covetousness, for one's life does not consist in the abundance of his possessions" (12:15). As Jesus had just seen with his own eyes, when life is money and money is life, division and conflict are inevitable. Greed turns people against one another. When our life is about money, money will take our life.

Love of money returns hate for many.

Isn't conflict a price worth paying if it means I'll be rich?

Greed Damns 12:16–21

"And he told them a parable, saying, 'The land of a rich man produced plentifully, and he thought to himself, "What shall I do, for I have nowhere to store my crops?"'" (12:16–17). He has so much, he doesn't know what to do with it all.

So, he decided to give away the excess to help the poor, right? No, he did the opposite. "And he said, 'I will do this: I will tear down my barns and build larger ones, and there I will store all my grain and my goods'" (12:18). Then he indulges in some back-slapping of his own back. "And I will say to my soul, 'Soul, you have ample goods laid up for many years; relax, eat, drink, be merry'" (12:19). It's party time! Money, money, money! Party, party, party! Sounds like the life most people want to live, doesn't it? It's a dream come true.

But God spoils the party and turns the dream into a nightmare. "Fool!" said God. "This night your soul is required of you, and the things you have prepared, whose will they be?" (12:20). Everyone called him wise, but God called him "fool." Everyone said he was a success, but God said he was a failure. He had his life all planned out, but God tore up his plans. He had prepared to live but had not prepared to die. He was a self-made man but became a self-destroyed man. He'd laid up treasure for himself but not for God (12:21). He had riches on earth but none in heaven. On earth he was a billionaire, but in heaven he was bankrupt.

If I make life about money, money will take my life.

Changing Our Story with God's Story

Our merciful Savior told this story to change our stories. "So is the one who lays up treasure for himself and is not rich toward God" (12:21). A life of riches is contrasted with a life rich toward God. As I discovered in my greedy twenties, if we want to change our relationship with money, we need to change our relationship with God. A rich relationship with God replaces a poor relationship with money.

Summary: What happens when money is life and life is money? Conflict and condemnation. Therefore, *invest in the eternal God for eternal love and eternal life.*

Question: How are you investing in God today?

Prayer: Rich God, thank you for satisfying me. Help me to invest in you so that I can enjoy true and eternal riches.

The unprepared will not be unpunished.

22

Are You Ready for a Reward?

LUKE 12:35-48

"Dad, if your family never visited us, our house would fall apart." That's what my kids used to say about the busy two or three days of repairing, decorating, tidying, and cleaning just before my family would visit us from the UK. It would be all-hands-on-deck for a couple of crazy days, and we usually just finished everything the second before our relatives arrived.

My kids were probably right. Without the expectation of visitors arriving, we would have kept putting off the work. Knowing my parents or siblings would show up in a day or two got us motivated and moving. In Luke 12:35–48, Jesus appeals to that motivation to get us ready for his arrival at the end of time by providing two answers to the question: *Why should we get ready for the end?*

The Ready Will Be Rewarded 12:35-44

The Lord begins by describing servants who are prepared for their master's arrival. They don't know when he's coming, therefore they're always ready for his knock (12:36–37).

It's a lot of work to be permanently and perfectly organized for a visitor who could come at any moment. He therefore rewards them with a blessing when they open the door. Instead of going straight to bed, the master puts on his apron, invites his servants to recline at the table, and serves them supper (12:37)! Truly,

"Blessed are those servants whom the master finds awake when he comes" (12:37).

Jesus is the Master and we are his servants in this story. Therefore, "You also must be ready, for the Son of Man is coming at an hour you do not expect" (12:40). What a reward for readiness! Jesus will serve his servants.

But there's more. When Peter asks if the story is really about them (12:41), Jesus confirms it is and promises the additional reward of opportunities for even greater service: "Truly, I say to you, he will set him over all his possessions" (12:44). The servant will serve his servants and give them even greater service. What a merciful Master!

Readiness is rewarded.

What happens if I don't get ready?

The Unprepared Will Be Punished 12:45–48

An unfaithful servant takes advantage of the master's delay by abusing the master's servants and property. But one day, the unfaithful servant hears a familiar knock at the door. He stops in his tracks and rushes to put everything right. But it's too late. The result? "The master . . . will cut him in pieces and put him with the unfaithful. And that servant who knew his master's will but did not get ready or act according to his will, will receive a severe beating" (12:46–47).

And just in case someone says, "That's not fair to the poor servant," Jesus assures us of his perfect justice. The unfaithful who knew God's will, will be punished more than the unfaithful who didn't (12:47–48). "Everyone to whom much was given, of him much will be required, and from him to whom they entrusted much, they will demand the more" (12:48). When Jesus punishes, it's perfect punishment. How much the unfaithful know decides how much they are punished.

The unprepared will not be unpunished.

Changing Our Story with God's Story

Jesus told this story to change our story both during time and at the end of time. Although there's a warning for the unfaithful in his Story, the greater part is two motivations to faithfulness: Jesus will serve us and give us greater service. Readiness will have real rewards.

Summary: Why should we get ready for the end? *Get ready for the end because readiness for the end decides our end.*

Question: How will Jesus's future service of you change the way you serve him today?

Prayer: Master, I am your faithful servant. Make me ready for your return so that your return will be rewarding.

Suffer for Jesus now, or suffer without Jesus forever.

23

Suffer to Save

LUKE 12:49–59

Suffering is at the heart of the gospel. But many rip the heart of suffering out of the gospel. They want a painless cross, a painless Christian life, and a painless eternity for everyone. They want to cover up the truths of Christ's suffering on the cross, the Christian's suffering in life, and the Christless suffering in hell. Attempting to make the gospel more palatable and popular, they end up with no gospel at all.

Why do we insist that suffering is at the heart of the gospel? Let's hear from Jesus in Luke 12:49–59.

Jesus Will Suffer for People 12:49–50

Why did Jesus come to this world? Jesus answers: "I came to cast fire on the earth, and would that it were already kindled!" (12:49). Jesus was not looking and longing for the day of judgment here, but for the day of Pentecost, a day when tongues of fire pictured gospel preaching burning up sin and evil (Acts 2:3).

But, before that fire, there had to be a baptism. "I have a baptism to be baptized with, and how great is my distress until it is accomplished!" (12:50). The military used the word *baptize* to describe the overwhelming destruction of a city. Paul used this meaning of *baptism* in Romans 6:3 and Colossians 2:12 to depict the putting to death of an old way of life. Jesus suffered the baptism of overwhelming destruction to put to death the old way of life of his baptized people. That's why he said, "How great is my distress until it is accomplished!" (12:50).

Jesus was destroyed to destroy our sin.

What an amazing message: Jesus suffered for sinners. Surely everyone is going to love Jesus for that, right?

People Will Suffer for Jesus 12:51-59

"Do you think that I have come to give peace on earth? No, I tell you, but rather division" (12:51). People will fight the gospel rather than have faith in it. Instead of turning to the Lord, people will turn against those who turn to the Lord. "From now on in one house there will be five divided, three against two and two against three. They will be divided, father against son and son against father, mother against daughter and daughter against mother . . ." (12:52–53). The gospel of peace starts war. The gospel of love stirs up hate. Those who bring the good news will be treated badly.

Despite the massive and momentous signs of Christ's baptism of suffering, the outpouring of the Holy Spirit, and the power of gospel preaching, most will not recognize or understand these gospel signs. They could figure out what the clouds and wind predicted but couldn't figure out what Jesus was predicting (12:54–56).

Gospel signs come with gospel suffering.

What happens to those who reject Jesus's signs?

People Will Suffer without Jesus 12:57-59

Jesus will suffer for people, people will suffer for Jesus, and people will suffer without Jesus. He warns those who are massively indebted to God to find a way of paying off their debts "lest he drag you to the judge, and the judge hand you over to the officer, and the officer put you in prison. I tell you, you will never get out until you have paid the very last penny" (12:58–59). Settle your debts with God now, or you'll be paying them off forever.

Suffer for Jesus now, or suffer without Jesus forever.

Changing Our Story with God's Story

Change your story by believing Jesus suffered in your place, by suffering for Jesus, and by warning the Christless about eternal suffering.

Summary: Why do we insist that suffering is at the heart of the gospel story? *Tell the story of suffering, or there will be no story of blessing.*

Question: If Jesus has suffered for you, how will you suffer for Jesus so that others don't suffer without Jesus?

Prayer: Suffering Savior, I confess my sins caused your suffering. May your saving suffering make me willing to endure short suffering so that others can be saved from eternal suffering.

Great repentance saves from the greatest tragedy.

24

Tragedies Are Teachers

LUKE 13:1-5

Bad events can be good teachers. When I was twenty years old, the Chernobyl Nuclear Power Plant exploded in what was then the Soviet Union. Although the Russians tried to keep the catastrophe secret for days, a huge cloud of radioactive particles began to spread over Europe.

Experts predicted hundreds of thousands of cancer deaths over the coming years. It was a scary time. A few days after the explosion, I got soaked in an unexpected rain shower on the way to catch a bus to work. Dripping wet, I got on the bus and opened my morning paper, which greeted me with a government warning: "Radiation cloud over UK. Stay indoors and avoid rain!"

I wasn't a Christian at the time, but this got me thinking seriously about my life and my death, which I was pretty sure was imminent. It made me think about what would happen to me after death. This bad event was a good teacher for me.

But bad events can also be bad teachers, as we'll discover in Luke 13:1-5.

How do we use bad events as good teachers instead of bad teachers?

Let Jesus teach us how.

Tragic Events Cause Tragic Reasoning 13:1-5

Jesus was asked about some Galilean Jews who were offering their sacrifices in the temple when they were suddenly and cruelly executed under Pilate's orders.

Jesus's compassionate response reveals that behind the people's report of this tragic event was a tragic theology. "He answered them, 'Do you think that these Galileans were worse sinners than all the other Galileans, because they suffered in this way? No, I tell you'" (13:2–3). This tragic event caused tragic reasoning, that is, extraordinary disasters are the result of extraordinary sins. Some had concluded that these Galilean Jews had suffered a terrible death because they had committed terrible sins. "No, I tell you," Jesus asserted.

Jesus reminded them of a tragedy closer to home that involved not just the common Galileans but the elite Jerusalemites. "Those eighteen on whom the tower in Siloam fell and killed them: do you think that they were worse offenders than all the others who lived in Jerusalem? No, I tell you" (13:4–5). Jesus's Q&A session exposed their tragic reasoning that big sufferings are always the result of big sins.

Here's how to think about tragedies. Jesus said, "Unless you repent, you will all likewise perish" (13:3). And, just in case we missed it the first time, Jesus says it a second time: "Unless you repent, you will all likewise perish" (13:5).

Big pains don't always mean big sins.

So, how should we think about tragedies?

Tragic Events Save from a Tragic Future

Don't think about others' sins; think about your own. Don't just look back on tragic deaths; look ahead to your own death. Don't use tragedy to look down on people; use it to look up to God. Don't turn a tragedy into a reason for pride, but a reason for penitence. Use world tragedies to avoid an eternal tragedy. The greatest tragedy is not losing your life but losing your soul.

Great repentance saves from the greatest tragedy.

Changing Our Story with God's Story

Every story of tragedy is an opportunity to change our story into one with a happy ending. Although our first instinct may be to think about the victims' sins, it is best to turn our attention to turning from our sins. If bad events turn us from our sin, we turn bad events into good teachers.

Summary: How do we use bad events as good teachers instead of bad teachers? *Use tragedies to teach repentance and so avoid the greatest tragedy.*

Question: Who and how can you help to turn tragedies into teachers today?

Prayer: God of Providence, we all deserve to die because of our sins. Therefore, when I hear of tragic deaths, give me repentance to turn from my sins and keep me from thinking I'm better than those who died. I praise you that I can escape the greatest tragedy by simple repentance and faith in Jesus.

Fruitless faith is fatal faith.

25

Fertilizing Faith

LUKE 13:6–17

An apple-free apple tree is a dead apple tree. Fruit-free faith is fatal faith. An apple tree without apples and faith without fruit are worse than useless. Both are a waste of time and space. However, before they're cut down and replaced, there's one more option that can fertilize the deadest to life. *What is faith's fertilizer?* Jesus points the fruitless to himself in Luke 13:6–17.

Dead Faith Is Dangerous Faith 13:6–9

"A man had a fig tree planted in his vineyard, and he came seeking fruit on it and found none. And he said to the vinedresser, 'Look, for three years now I have come seeking fruit on this fig tree, and I find none. Cut it down. Why should it use up the ground?'" (13:6–7).

This fig tree is in great danger. Fruitless for three years, its owner is ready to chop it down and replace it with a fig tree that actually produces figs. Three years is plenty of time to grow a fig. As my green-thumbed daughter-in-law reminds me when I'm impatiently waiting for my garden to grow: "The first year the plants sleep, the second year they creep, and the third year they leap."

At the end of year three, this fig tree still hasn't gotten out of bed, and the fig farmer is at the end of his patience. While he's sharpening his axe, one of his workers pleads for one more year. "Sir, let it alone this year also, until I dig around it and put on manure. Then if it should bear fruit next year, well and good; but if not, you can cut it down" (13:8–9).

As we'll see shortly, this is a story about faith not figs. Israel's faith is dead, lifeless, and useless. Jesus came looking for fruit and found next to nothing. He came as the final fertilizer, the nation's last chance for the dangerously barren to be spiritually fruitful.

Fruitless faith is fatal faith.

If my faith is dead and fruitless, how do I get life and fruit?

Living Faith Is Saving Faith 13:10–17

Luke provides a real-life example of dead and fruitless faith contrasted with living and fruitful faith. One Sabbath, Jesus healed a woman who had been disabled for eighteen years. "He laid his hands on her, and immediately she was made straight, and she glorified God" (13:13).

And everyone rejoiced and worshiped with her? Not exactly. The ruler of the synagogue was furious that Jesus had "worked," and rebuked the woman for being healed on the Sabbath day. "Indignant because Jesus had healed on the Sabbath, he said to the people, 'There are six days in which work ought to be done. Come on those days and be healed, and not on the Sabbath day'" (13:14).

Jesus called out his horrible hypocrisy by exposing how this religious ruler watered his thirsty donkey on the Sabbath but stopped the healing of disabled people on the Sabbath. He cared more for his donkeys than for the disabled (13:15–16). But not Jesus. Listen to his merciful defense of the healed woman: "Ought not this woman, a daughter of Abraham whom Satan bound for eighteen years, be loosed from this bond on the Sabbath day?" (13:16).

"As he said these things, all his adversaries were put to shame, and all the people rejoiced at all the glorious things that were done by him" (13:17). The spiritually dead died deeper, but living faith was fertilized by Jesus to bear even more fruit of public joyful praise.

Jesus enabled the spiritually disabled.

Changing Our Story with God's Story

If you're worried that your faith is fruitless, Jesus has come to you today to give you additional time and additional fertilizer. Use this parable and event to see the danger of deadness and get faith fertilizer from Jesus.

Summary: What is faith's fertilizer? *Ask Jesus to fertilize your faith so that you produce joyful and juicy fruit.*

Question: What spiritual fruit will you cultivate today and give to others to enjoy?

Prayer: Heavenly Farmer, fertilize my fruit to assure me that my faith is living and to bring joy to your church and glory to your name.

Recliners will be restless forever, but strivers will recline forever.

Hear
God's Story | Change
Your Story | Tell
the Story | Change
Others' Stories

26

How Many Will Be Saved?

LUKE 13:22-30

The wrong question gets the wrong answer. If we ask the wrong question, we'll get the wrong answer. The devil loves to get us asking the wrong questions because he loves wrong answers. He especially loves when asking wrong questions keeps us from the most important questions.

In Luke 13:22-30, someone asked Jesus the wrong question: "Lord, will those who are saved be few?" (13:23). How did Jesus handle it? He gave the right question so we get the right answer. The right question is not "Lord how many will be saved?" but "Will I be saved?" The former question is speculative and secondary. The right question is personal and primary. Jesus not only gave the right question; he also gave hints to help us arrive at the right answer.

The Saved Are Striving 13:24

"Strive to enter through the narrow door. For many, I tell you, will seek to enter and will not be able" (13:24). "Wait, I thought salvation was a resting not a striving." Striving is not the cause of salvation, but it does prove salvation. It doesn't start salvation, but it does accompany it. Resting in Christ is so hard for us that we have to strive for it.

Jesus was speaking to Jews who were resting in their national identity for salvation. The speculative questioner was typical of a complacent nation. So confident of their salvation, they spent their time hypothesizing about how many might possibly be saved.

Out of concern for their souls, Jesus challenged their smug self-confidence. He stirred them up with the difficulty of salvation (it's a "narrow door"), the attitude that escorts salvation ("striving," which means "agonizing"), and the warning that half-hearted seeking will not secure salvation: "For many, I tell you, will seek to enter and will not be able" (13:24).

We must strive to rest in Jesus.

What will happen at the end?
That's the next question and answer in Jesus's catechism.

The Saved Are Surprising 13:25–30

Jesus comes to close the door of time, leaving many standing outside banging on it and shouting, "Lord, open to us." He replies, "I do not know where you come from" (13:25). Shocked, they protest their entitlement: "We ate and drank in your presence, and you taught in our streets" (13:26). Not much striving there, is there?

His response stuns them: "'Depart from me, all you workers of evil!' In that place there will be weeping and gnashing of teeth, when you see Abraham and Isaac and Jacob and all the prophets in the kingdom of God but you yourselves cast out" (13:27–28). Workers of evil are those who don't rest in Christ. If we're not resting in Christ, all our works are evil in God's sight. Good works start with a good rest. No rest in Christ means no rest in hell, a restlessness made worse by seeing Gentile resters resting in the kingdom.

"And people will come from east and west, and from north and south, and recline at table in the kingdom of God. And behold, some are last who will be first, and some are first who will be last" (13:29–30). The last to hear about salvation (the Gentiles) win it; the first to hear about salvation (the Jews) lose it. The Gentiles are surprised to receive salvation; the Jews are surprised at losing it.

Recliners will be restless forever, but strivers will recline forever.

Changing Our Story with God's Story

Use this story to stir up your story. Strive to rest in Christ alone, to recline in heaven never alone. Use the prospect of relaxing forever with Abraham, Isaac, and Jacob in the kingdom to make you run to Christ today. Make sure your surprise is not that you're unsaved, but that you're saved

Summary: How many will be saved? *Just make sure you will be saved.*

Question: How hard are you working to rest in Christ, and what's keeping you from it?

Prayer: Surprising God, thank you for surprising me with salvation by rest. Help me to work at resting better in Christ.

Don't hate too late, or you'll be too late for love.

27

A Lover for Haters

LUKE 13:31–35

Lovers of Jesus are hated for Jesus. You've experienced that, haven't you? You meet people who are Christless and hopeless. You love them, tell them about Christ's love, and they hate you for it. They even accuse *you* of being a hater. You're like, "What just happened? All I did was love them, and they hated me for it."

How should we respond to those who hate us for loving them? Sometimes we're tempted to hate the haters, aren't we? Or, at least, to stop loving those who don't want to be loved. Or maybe we start editing the good news to make it more acceptable. But then we all lose. Jesus was the greatest lover who suffered the greatest hate, and he models how to love haters in Luke 13:31–35.

Jesus Is Hated 13:31–33

The Pharisees hated Jesus because his purity shone a bright light on their hypocrisy and therefore threatened their power. So, when he started heading toward their power HQ, Jerusalem, they tried to scare him away by telling him that Herod wanted to kill him (13:31). Undaunted, Jesus replied, "Go and tell that fox, 'Behold, I cast out demons and perform cures today and tomorrow, and the third day I finish my course. Nevertheless, I must go on my way today and tomorrow and the day following, for it cannot be that a prophet should perish away from Jerusalem'" (13:32–33). Refusing to be intimidated by the haters, and by the hating devil behind them all, his love pressed on to the epicenter of hate.

Haters gonna hate, because the devil's gonna devil.

Can't I just do loving actions?
Do I really need love in my heart for haters?

Jesus Loves Haters 13:34

Loving actions cannot be sustained without a loving heart, as Jesus shows when he laments, "O Jerusalem, Jerusalem, the city that kills the prophets and stones those who are sent to it! How often would I have gathered your children together as a hen gathers her brood under her wings, and you were not willing!" (13:34). Surrounded by hungry foxes, this beautiful hen reveals a beautiful heart. There's no anger here, only compassion and pity for what they were missing out on. Seeing the danger they were in, he extended his loving wings to offer them warm, inviting, protective love. Their response? "Chop off his wings."

A loving hen invites foxes to be her chicks.

So, do we just keep offering love to haters and
never warn them of the consequences?

Jesus Will Judge Haters 13:35

Having lovingly headed into the storm of hate, and lovingly offered the haters salvation yet again, Jesus lovingly warned them of where their hate would end up. "Behold, your house is forsaken. And I tell you, you will not see me until you say, 'Blessed is he who comes in the name of the Lord!'" (13:35). You'll destroy me, but your HQ of hate will be destroyed, and your heart of hate will eventually be forced to admit that I did come in the name of the Lord. But too late for love.

Don't hate too late, or you'll be too late for love.

Changing Our Story with God's Story

One of the best ways that I've found to help me love my haters is to remember how Jesus loved me into his love. I was one of the foxes, and his loving invitation turned me into one of his chicks. Therefore, I try to follow his example and extend Christ's wings to the foxes around me.

Summary: How should we respond to those who hate us for loving them? *Ask for the heart of Jesus so that we can respond like Jesus, with loving actions, words, and warnings.*

Question: Which hater will you love today?

Prayer: Great Lover, I was a hater you changed into a lover, therefore help me to extend your love to my haters so that you can turn them into lovers.

Give up to
go up.

 Hear
God's Story | Change
Your Story | Tell
the Story | Change
Others' Stories

28

Gospel Manners

LUKE 14:7–24

We've all done it, haven't we? We've embarrassed ourselves in a social situation by breaking some mysterious rule of etiquette. At best, people just laugh or frown at us. But sometimes a faux pas is so serious that you get ejected and excluded. Manners matter.

What about gospel manners? *What are gospel manners, and how do we observe them?* In Luke 14:7–24 Jesus invites us to three feasts to teach us three rules of gospel etiquette. In his kind pity, he wants to help us avoid spiritual embarrassment, ejection, and exclusion when invited to the gospel banquet.

Come Humbly 14:7–11

Have you ever sat in the wrong seat and been asked to move? Mortifying, isn't it? We meet a fellow sufferer in 14:7–11. But don't sympathize with him, because he deserved the reddest of faces. Mr. First maneuvered his way to the best seat in the house. But just when he was getting comfortable, the host asked him to give up his seat for the guest of honor. All eyes were on him as he was forced out of the seat of honor. Worse, by that time the only seat left was the lowest one (14:7–9). Mr. First was now Mr. Last. How embarrassing!

Gospel manners are: take the lowest seat, and you'll be asked to go up to a higher seat. Follow this protocol and "You will be honored in the presence of all who sit at table with you. For everyone who exalts himself will be humbled, and he who humbles himself will be exalted" (14:10–11).

Give up to go up.

Who else is going to be there? You might be disappointed.

Come Empty 14:12–14

One of the most stressful parts of wedding planning is who to invite, or rather, who to offend. We can't offend family, so they've all got to come. We can't offend rich Auntie Gertrude if we want to retire early. And we'd really like to go our neighbor's wedding in a few months, so we'd better invite them.

That's a perfectly understandable invitation strategy, but it's not a gospel strategy. The gospel banquet is for those who cannot pay back. It's given to those who cannot give anything in return. It's for the empty. Therefore, "invite the poor, the crippled, the lame, the blind, and you will be blessed, because they cannot repay you. For you will be repaid at the resurrection of the just" (14:13–14).

Come empty to be filled.

"I'm not sure I can make it. My schedule is rather full."
You need to clear your schedule.

Come Immediately 14:15–24

The third feast was a big letdown. The invitation said, "Come, for everything is now ready" (14:17). And everyone stampeded in the opposite direction. "They all alike began to make excuses" (14:18). The different excuses were really one excuse: "I'm too busy at the moment."

Instead of canceling the event, though, the Master told his servant, "Go out quickly to the streets and lanes of the city, and bring in the poor and crippled and blind and lame" (14:21). The house filled up quickly. The too-busy-for-a-banquet crowd was sweating in the fields, while the destitute, diseased, and disabled were being wined and dined in a mansion (14:24). What a sight that party must have been. No photographers from *People* magazine there though.

Say a quick "yes" to God, to avoid God's long "no."

Changing Our Story with God's Story

Let's not only save ourselves eternal embarrassment by observing gospel manners, but encourage and exhort others to do the same. Because manners matter, find God's ways to overcome pride, self-sufficiency, delaying tactics, and excuses.

Summary: What are gospel manners, and how do we observe them? *Avoid gospel embarrassment, ejection, and exclusion by coming humbly, empty, and immediately.*

Question: Whom can you invite to the gospel banquet today, and how will you word the invitation to maximize its attractiveness?

Prayer: Heavenly Host, thank you so much for your gospel invitation, which I heartily and humbly accept. Use me to invite others to join me at the gospel table today.

God's finding begins long before he finds us.

29

Lost and Found

LUKE 15

I'm great at losing things but terrible at finding things. Half my life is spent asking my wife, "Shona, have you seen my wallet/phone/keys/belt/charger?" and so on. And she always finds what I've spent ages looking for. (I still secretly think she hides my stuff so she can "miraculously" find it.) In our house, I'm known as the loser and Shona is the finder.

In Luke 15, three parables answer a basic spiritual question: *"Who are the lost and who is the finder?"* Let's focus on the parable of the lost son to get our answer.[1]

We Are the Lost 15:12–14

Come with me inside the head and heart of this lost young man.

I'm fed up (15:12): "Dad's a good guy, but life here is so boring. That's all going to change today. I'm going to ask Dad for an advance on my inheritance, and then I'll be off to a bigger and better life in the city."

I'm free (15:13): "I can't believe it! I'm on the road. Free. At. Last. No more Sunday worship, no more family devotions, no more 'Home by midnight,' no more boredom. Free to choose my friends, free to try whatever I want, free to be me. Freedom! Watch out world, here I come!"

I'm famished (15:13–14): "I'm sure I had more money in that bag. Where did it go? I couldn't have spent it already, could I? Where are

---

1   Much of this chapter first appeared in my article "The Prodigal Son," Ligonier.org, November 25, 2012, https://www.ligonier.org. © Ligonier Ministries 2012. Used by permission of Ligonier Ministries. All rights reserved.

my friends? I haven't seen anyone since I started having to cut back last week. I'm so hungry. How can I get something to eat?"

Lostness is emptiness.

How can I get found?

God Is the Finder 15:15–24

God's finding of this lost young man began in a pigsty.

I'm filthy (15:15–16): "I can't believe this. From the beautiful people to pigs! From parties to a pigsty! I never thought pig slops could look so tasty. Some friends they were—wouldn't even help me through my little downturn. They make me sick. The pigs make me sick. I make myself sick. What can I do? What a mess!"

I'm foolish (15:17): "What am I doing? Look at what I've given up. And look at what I've 'gained.' I've been such a fool. Come on, think, man. Even Dad's servants have a better life than this. They've got plenty of food, and I'm simply starving. Maybe I should. . . . No . . . I couldn't. I couldn't."

I'm finished (15:18): "OK, I'm done. I can't take any more of this. I'll go home, ask Dad for forgiveness, beg for mercy, and hope he takes me on as a servant."

I'm forgiven (15:20–24): "Who's that on the hill? Looks like Dad looking for one of his lost sheep. Oh, now he's running . . . in this direction. I wonder if he saw me?"

"My son, my son, my son. Welcome home, my son, my son."

"Dad, please don't call me your son. I don't deserve that. I am so, so sorry. I've sinned against God and I've sinned against you. I know I don't deserve this, but if I could even be one of your servants, that would be huge."

"Servant? Never, never, never. You're my son. Always and ever my son."

"No, Dad. It's not right."

"If you want justice, you've come to the wrong place, my son. You were lost and dead. I've found you alive. You most certainly are and shall be my son. We're going to celebrate and have such a good time."

God's finding begins long before he finds us.

Changing Our Story with God's Story

Our merciful Father finds us by making us see how filthy and foolish we are, and by giving us the desire to finish with sin and seek his forgiveness. When these things are happening in us, the finder is already on his way.

Summary: Who are the lost and who is the finder? *Confess we are the lost and God is the finder and celebrate his finding of all his lost ones.*

Question: Which prodigal will you pray for today, and how is your prayer shaped by this parable?

Prayer: Flawless Finder, please find my prodigal.

Unless God is worth everything, everything is worth nothing.

30

Praise the Appraiser

LUKE 16:14–31

A good appraiser should be praised. Recently, one of my friends had his property appraised, and the appraisal value was way below what he'd hoped for, making it impossible for him to get a mortgage. Initially, he and his wife were deeply disappointed, but before long they realized the appraiser had actually done them a favor. He saved them a lot of money and stress in the long run.

When it comes to life, *who is the most reliable appraiser?* Luke 14:19–31 gives us zero stars but God five stars.

We Are Bad Appraisers 16:14–19

"What is exalted among men is an abomination in the sight of God" (16:15). What people value most, God values least. What do people put the highest value on today? Much the same as in Jesus's day: lots of money (16:14), lots of sex (16:18), and lots of celebrity lifestyle (16:19).

Jesus tore off the massive price tags people put on money, sex, and lifestyle, and replaced them with his own valuation. Zero. Unless God is valued most, everything is worth nothing. That appraisal may leave you disappointed for a time, but better that than disappointment for all eternity.

Unless God is worth everything, everything is worth nothing.

Who then is a reliable appraiser?

God Is the Best Appraiser 16:19–31

Two very different men led two very different lives. "There was a rich man who was clothed in purple and fine linen and who feasted sumptuously every day. And at his gate was laid a poor man named Lazarus, covered with sores, who desired to be fed with what fell from the rich man's table. Moreover, even the dogs came and licked his sores" (16:19–21).

There's no question who's living the life worth living here, is there? It's Mr. Rich and Famous, right? That's our appraisal. But their deaths reveal God's appraisal. Though Lazarus was poor in wealth, he was rich in faith and went straight to heaven. From the worst poverty to the greatest riches—quicker than you can blink.

Mr. Rich went to sleep one night, and the next time he opened his eyes he saw the flaming walls of hell (16:23). From money, sex, and the celebrity lifestyle to eternal hell, eternal torments, and eternal thirst.

There he continued to treat Lazarus like a servant, and angrily argued with God. But heaven replied: "Child, remember that you in your lifetime received your good things, and Lazarus in like manner bad things; but now he is comforted here, and you are in anguish" (16:25). You did your own appraisal instead of asking God for his. Now there's no way back, there's no do-over. "Between us and you a great chasm has been fixed, in order that those who would pass from here to you may not be able, and none may cross from there to us" (16:26). The final exam is final.

Though too late, Mr. Rich realized that he had put the wrong price tag on everything and now wanted Lazarus to go warn his family: "Don't do what I did." Heaven said, "They have Moses and the Prophets; let them hear them" (16:29).

God's reliable word is God's reliable appraiser.

Changing Our Story with God's Story

We not only have Moses and the prophets; we have Jesus and the apostles. Let's hear them and trust their valuations. Put the highest value on God, and let him value everything else. Then we'll avoid joining Mr. Rich in hell and ensure we spend eternity with Lazarus in heaven.

Summary: Who is the most reliable appraiser? *Trust God's appraisals found in his word.*

Question: What are you tempted to appraise too highly, and how will you praise what God appraises highest?

Prayer: Accurate Appraiser, make me share in your valuations so that I will be eternally rich rather than eternally poor.

Our sins multiply others' sins.

31

Relational Faith

LUKE 17:1-6

The Christian faith is a social faith. It was never meant to be lived out alone, but always in community with others. God designed the fellowship of believers as a help to our faith, but that also brings some difficulties we wouldn't face if we were Christian hermits.

Sometimes people and situations are so challenging and complicated that we want to transfer our membership to Recluse Church. But there is no such church, and we therefore have to face relational challenges with God's help. *What are some of the relational challenges in Christianity, and how do we overcome them?* Jesus answers in Luke 17:1–6.

When We Sin, We Tempt Others to Sin 17:1-2

Sin multiplies sin. How so? Sometimes, our sin plants the thought of sin in others' minds. Or the thought was already there, but our sin gives others permission or encouragement to give in to the temptation. Or maybe we provoke people to sin by our sinning against them. Sin never exists alone but always reproduces.

Sin breeds sin, and causing someone else to sin is more serious than we might think. As Jesus said, "Temptations to sin are sure to come, but woe to the one through whom they come! It would be better for him if a millstone were hung around his neck and he were cast into the sea than that he should cause one of these little ones to sin" (17:1–2). Or to put it in more modern terms: it would be better to have the mafia fit you for concrete boots than to tempt someone to sin.

Our sins multiply others' sins.

I'll try not to make others sin, but they'll do that without my help anyway. What do I do then?

When Others Sin, We Forgive Their Sin 17:3–5

When Jesus cautions, "Pay attention to yourselves!" (17:3), he's not just warning us against making others sin. He's also admonishing us to be forgivers of others' sins. "If your brother sins, rebuke him, and if he repents, forgive him, and if he sins against you seven times in the day, and turns to you seven times, saying, 'I repent,' you must forgive him" (17:3–4).

Jesus fills in three holes we often fall into when it comes to forgiveness. The first pitfall is our tendency to ignore or excuse sin. Jesus shovels in this truth: "If your brother sins, rebuke him." Although we can overlook small sins (Prov. 19:11), we don't have this option when it's anything serious. We must address it and call the sinner to repentance.

The second pothole is forgiving without repentance. Jesus levels that hole with: "If he repents, forgive him." God is our model forgiver, and he forgives only upon repentance (Eph. 4:32). We don't do anyone any favors by forgiving when they don't want to be truly forgiven.

The third crater is limited forgiveness. Jesus pours in this cement: "If he sins against you seven times in the day, and turns to you seven times, saying, 'I repent,' you must forgive him" (17:4). *Seven* is often used in the Bible for perfection or completeness, therefore Jesus is not saying forgiveness runs out on sin number eight. He's calling us to complete forgiveness.

It's not surprising that after Jesus warned against making others sin and then called us to forgive others' sin, the disciples replied: "Increase our faith!" (17:5). They realized that this was humanly impossible—but not gospel impossible.

More faith in the gospel makes sin stoppable and forgivable.

Changing Our Story with God's Story

Although we sometimes think a reclusive life will increase and improve our faith, Jesus says that, in truth, a *relational* life will, because it makes us need and ask for more faith. Jesus calls us to a relational story, not a reclusive story.

Summary: What are some of the relational challenges in Christianity, and how do we overcome them? *Believe more to sin less, and believe more to forgive more.*

Question: Whom do you need to forgive, and whom do you need to ask for forgiveness?

Prayer: Holy God, you are also a forgiving God. Give me your holiness and forgiveness so that I don't make others sin and so that I forgive others' sins.

A lowly heart raises high thanks.

32

Grace Grows Gratitude

LUKE 17:11-19

Grace grows gratitude. If we haven't gotten grace, we won't give gratitude. Though I don't think the situation is as bad in the US, I find that gratitude seems to be dying in the UK. When my wife and I would give birthday or wedding gifts there, we received virtually no response. No excitement, no joy, no appreciation.

We eventually realized that it was connected with the decline of the gospel of grace. *How are grace and gratitude connected, and how can we use each to increase the other?* Turn to Luke 17:11-19 for the answer.

Gratitude Is Loud 17:11-15

As Jesus entered a village one day, ten lepers saw him and started crying out, "Jesus, Master, have mercy on us" (17:13). Instead of healing them immediately, he instructed them: "'Go and show yourselves to the priests.' And as they went, they were cleansed" (17:14).

So, they all ran back to Jesus and thanked him for his magnificent mercy, right? Nope! "One of them, when he saw that he was healed, turned back, praising God with a loud voice" (17:15). This solitary leper didn't hold back when it came to giving thanks. The word *loud* here means "mega." This was *mega*thanks.

A megahealing should produce megagratitude.

If there's volume on the outside, what turns the dial up on the inside? Humility.

Gratitude Is Lowly 17:16

The grateful leper "fell on his face at Jesus' feet, giving him thanks" (17:16). That's the secret to gratitude right there. Humility. We usually thank someone when we are accepting a gift rather than earning a reward. We acknowledge that someone gave us something we didn't have before. Gratitude says, "You're the giver, I'm the receiver." Gratitude is also a denial of entitlement. It's saying, "You didn't need to give that, and I didn't have any right to get it."

Significantly, the only leper who gave thanks was a Samaritan. Like most Jews of that day, the nine Jewish lepers felt entitled to God's blessings. They were healed and immediately thought, "Right, now back to rebuilding my life, my business, and my reputation." The thankful leper fell at Jesus's feet and humbly acknowledged that he did not deserve healing. He humbled himself and exalted God. God's reputation was first in his life.

A lowly heart raises high thanks.

Should I wait for others to give thanks before I do? If you do, you'll be waiting a long time!

Gratitude Is Lonely 17:17–19

"Jesus answered, 'Were not ten cleansed? Where are the nine? Was no one found to return and give praise to God except this foreigner?'" (17:17–18). All ten were lepers, all ten heard about Jesus, all ten believed he could help them, all ten asked for healing, all ten obeyed him, all ten went to the priests, and all ten were healed. When it came to gratitude though, the ten became one. One in ten, 10 percent, is probably about the same rate of gratitude today. Gratitude is lonely because faith is lonely. "Rise and go your way; your faith has made you well," explained Jesus (17:19). The man's believing attitude explained his growing gratitude.

Maximize faith to maximize gratitude.

Changing Our Story with God's Story

Like this leper, disregard whatever others are doing, and come to our merciful healer with loud thanks that grow out of a humble heart. As the Heidelberg Catechism frames it: guilt, grace, gratitude. When we see our guilt, we receive grace and express gratitude for God's salvation.

Summary: How are grace and gratitude connected, and how can we use grace to increase gratitude? *As grace grows gratitude, deepen your experience of grace to heighten your experience of gratitude.*

Question: How will you increase gratitude in your life, and whose lives will you change today by thanking them?

Prayer: Gracious God, I am a guilty leper, not deserving of the least of your mercies. Thank you for all your gifts, especially your gift of grace, and help me to live out my faith in grateful service.

The end times begin
with Christ's end,
but the end times end
with Christ's glory.

Hear
God's Story

Change
Your Story

Tell
the Story

Change
Others' Stories

33

The Beginning of the End

LUKE 17:20-37

The end of the world has started a lot of problems in the world. If you want to start an argument, start a conversation about how and when the world will end. "Don't worry, the world will never end," insist some. "Don't worry, we can interpret the end times and predict when it will be," others assure us. "We're all going to heaven anyway," say some, "so nothing to worry about at all." Who's right and who's wrong? *How should we view the end of the world?* Jesus has three answers in Luke 17:20-37.

The End Has Started 17:20-25

"When will the kingdom of God come?" the Pharisees asked Jesus. He replied, "The kingdom of God is not coming in ways that can be observed, nor will they say, 'Look, here it is!' or 'There!' for behold, the kingdom of God is in the midst of you" (17:20-22). The kingdom of God doesn't look like most kingdoms. Which is why the Pharisees didn't realize that the kingdom had already come and its king was standing right in front of them. When Jesus came, the kingdom came and the end times began.

Although the last days have begun, there will be many days when that will not be obvious (17:22). People will therefore make up their own stories about the end of the end times. "Don't listen to them," Jesus warns (17:23). They can predict the end about as well as someone can predict when and where lightning will strike (17:24). And anyway, before all that Jesus "must suffer many things and be rejected by this generation" (17:25).

The end times begin with Christ's end, but the end times end with Christ's glory.

Will anyone be able to forecast when these end times will end? No.

The End Will Surprise 17:26–33

The timing of the end of the end times will surprise many, just as the flood surprised most in Noah's day. "They were eating and drinking and marrying and being given in marriage, until the day when Noah entered the ark, and the flood came and destroyed them all" (17:27). The same thing happened when God judged Sodom (17:28–29). The same thing will happen when the Son of Man is revealed at the end of the end. People will be stunned and shocked at the timing. They will also be surprised at the speed of the last day. It will come so fast that no one will have time to put their house in order before appearing to answer God's summons (17:31–33).

When the end ends, it's the end.

But we'll all be saved anyway, right? Wrong.

The End Will Separate 17:34–37

One of the biggest mistakes people make about the end times is thinking that everyone will be saved. No, it will be a time of separating the saved from the unsaved: "I tell you, in that night there will be two in one bed. One will be taken and the other left. There will be two women grinding together. One will be taken and the other left." These shocking images disturbed his hearers who wanted to know more. "And they said to him, 'Where, Lord?' He said to them,

'Where the corpse is, there the vultures will gather'" (17:34–37). As birds of prey target dead corpses, so God's judgment targets the spiritually dead, Jesus warns.

Pray to God, or you'll be the prey of God.

Changing Our Story with God's Story

Knowing that we are already in the end times changes our relation to time. We realize time is short and eternity is long. However, it's better to think about the end times rather than forget them because then we will prepare by seeking until we find Christ's salvation.

Summary: How should we view the end of the world? *View the end of the world as already begun, as surprising in its timing and speed, and as a conclusive separator.*

Question: How many times did you think about the end yesterday? How will you remind yourself of the end more frequently today so you can be ready more consistently?

Prayer: Eternal God, you are without beginning and without end. But I have a beginning and end in this world. Prepare me for the end so that I will enjoy endless life rather than endless death.

Our character cuts prayer, but God's character cultivates prayer.

Hear
God's Story

Change
Your Story

Tell
the Story

Change
Others' Stories

34

Encouragement in Prayer

LUKE 18:1-8

When we're helpless, we ask help from the helpful. We don't ask a helpless person or an unhelpful person. We ask someone who we know is helpful. We weigh previous character when we're deciding whom to ask for help. When we need help around the house or in the yard, we know which kids will come running and which will walk away with a newly discovered limp.

In Luke 18:1–8, Jesus encourages us to keep asking God for help because of his proven character. Knowing his people will suffer discouraging persecution, "he told them a parable to the effect that they ought always to pray and not lose heart" (18:1). *What is it about God's character that can keep us praying without giving up?* Jesus wants us to think about ungodly character first of all.

Unjust Judges Act for Their Own Benefit 18:1-5

Widows have always been vulnerable to abuse, but it was especially bad in the Middle Eastern culture of Christ's day. Jesus had seen this many times and grieved over this terrible exploitation. One widow in particular got his sympathy, especially because the judge in her area was himself a wicked person. "He neither feared God nor respected man" (18:2). Despite this, she "kept coming to him and saying, 'Give me justice against my adversary'" (18:3).

"For a while he refused, but afterward he said to himself, 'Though I neither fear God nor respect man, yet because this widow keeps bothering me, I will give her justice, so that she will not beat me down by her continual coming'" (18:4–5). He gave her justice not because he was just, or because his ruling was just, but because he wanted peace and quiet.

Unjust judges do justice for unjust reasons.

Is there a just judge we can trust?

The Just Judge Acts for Our Benefit 18:6–8

Jesus said, "Hear what the unrighteous judge says" (18:6). He did justice despite his character. Therefore, how much more will a judge of just character give justice to the exploited and abused? "And will not God give justice to his elect, who cry to him day and night? Will he delay long over them? I tell you, he will give justice to them speedily" (18:7–8). God's just character should prompt prayer for justice. Unlike the unjust judge, God acts in the interests of victims, not for his own peace.

But there's a sting in the tail of this encouragement to pray: "Nevertheless, when the Son of Man comes, will he find faith on earth?" (18:8). The Lord is pictured as coming down to judge injustice, but where are those praying with faith in his just character?

Imagine the Supreme Court announces it will be visiting a small American town to hear any local cases, but no one turns up to present their case because no one really believed the Supreme Court was coming to town. Jesus is visiting town today. Will this Supreme Justice find any believers praying for justice? Delays in divine justice are usually a reflection of our character not God's.

Our character cuts prayer, but God's character cultivates prayer.

Changing Our Story with God's Story

Along with others, I suffered a grave injustice in January of 2000. Twenty-one years later, the primary perpetrators are still free and their victims still suffering. I've often given up praying for justice. But I've found that nothing stimulates prayer for justice like remembering the just character of the just God we pray to. His passion for justice can be triggered by faith in his justice. Let's take that faith to our own hearts and encourage it in the hearts of others.

Summary: What is it about God's character that motivates us to pray for justice without giving up? *Use God's just character to encourage persevering prayer for justice.*

Question: What situation of injustice are you facing, and how can you use God's character to encourage you?

Prayer: Just God, I love your justice and your passion for justice. I praise you that you are righting wrongs and one day will right all wrongs.

Go low to go high.

35

Whom Do You Trust?

LUKE 18:9–14

We're all trusters; it's just a question of whom do we trust. Even the most skeptical, doubtful, and suspicious people are trusters. It's just that they trust in themselves rather than anyone else. We can't stop ourselves from trusting—it's part of being human. All we can do is choose whom we trust. Trust is a decision, a choice, but it's also a feeling. It's a feeling of safety, of confidence, of certainty. So, whom do you trust? Especially, *whom do you trust when it comes to your salvation?*

Ultimately, there are only two choices when it comes to salvation, as Jesus demonstrates in Luke 18:9–14.

Self-Trust Is Self-Destruction 18:9–14

The Pharisee was *confident.* He represented those "who trusted in themselves that they were righteous" (18:9). He had great faith . . . in himself. Self-righteousness gave him self-confidence.

He was *conceited.* "The Pharisee, standing by himself, prayed" (18:11). This verse literally means that he prayed to himself. His prayer was addressed to God but never reached God. The Pharisee was praying to himself about himself. Asking for nothing, he congratulated himself and spent his time telling God what a good man he was.

He was *contemptuous.* He "treated others with contempt" (18:9), as we hear in his prayer: "God, I thank you that I am not like other men, extortioners, unjust, adulterers, or even like this tax collector.

I fast twice a week; I give tithes of all that I get" (18:11–12). He found worse men than himself, compared himself favorably with them, and looked down on them with contempt.

He was *condemned*. He went back home completely unjustified (18:14). He asked for nothing and got nothing. He went to church bad, but went home worse. He lifted himself up to God, but God dropped him back down again. "For everyone who exalts himself will be humbled" (18:14).

Go high to go low.

Whom do we trust if we want to be safe and feel safe?

Savior-Trust Is Salvation 18:13–14

Tax collectors were viewed as the lowest of the low, but Jesus raised this one high because he had a lowly heart.

He was *reverent*. "The tax collector, standing far off, would not even lift up his eyes to heaven" (18:13). Ashamed of himself and of his sins, he could barely set foot inside the temple door.

He was *repentant*. He "beat his breast" (lit., he "pounded on his chest repeatedly"), indicating his hatred of his horrible heart. While the Pharisee singled himself out as the holy one, the tax collector singled himself out as the unholy one. "God, be merciful to me, a sinner!"

He *requested*. The Pharisee asked for nothing and got nothing. In asking for mercy, the tax collector asked for everything. "God be merciful to me" can be translated "God make propitiation for me." He knew he needed a sacrifice to turn away God's anger.

He was *righteous*. He "went down to his house justified" (18:14). The Pharisee went home rejected and condemned by God, but the tax collector went home with God's acceptance and forgiveness. God declared him righteous. He fell before God, but God elevated him into communion with himself (18:14).

Go low to go high.

Changing Our Story with God's Story

One of these stories is our story. We're either trusting in ourselves or trusting in the Savior, trusting in our merit or trusting in God's mercy. Which feels safer to you? Which ending will your story have?

Summary: Whom do you trust when it comes to your salvation? *Trust the Savior not yourself, and you'll not only be saved, you'll feel saved.*

Question: Think of a time or situation where you trusted yourself and it turned out badly. How can you reduce self-trust and increase God-trust?

Prayer: Friend of Sinners, help me to trust 100 percent in you and 0 percent in myself or anyone else. God, be merciful to me a sinner.

Jesus invests everything in poor stocks in tough times.

Hear
God's Story

Change
Your Story

Tell
the Story

Change
Others' Stories

36

Start with the End in View

LUKE 19:11-27

Our view of the end of the world affects what we start in the world. If we think the end of the world is imminent, we're not going to start a business, enroll in college, build a house, or start a mission, are we? Instead, we'll do nothing and passively wait for the end. Such an unproductive eschatology (view of the end times) does not sound like the right eschatology, does it? So, *what's the proper and productive way to view the end?*

As Jesus approached Jerusalem in Luke 19:11-27, he realized that many of his followers "supposed that the kingdom of God was to appear immediately" (19:11). Knowing how this mistaken view would damage the kingdom's advance in the world, Jesus told them a parable to stir them out of passive waiting and into active mission.

Our Master Invests in Us 19:12-14

"He said therefore, 'A nobleman went into a far country to receive for himself a kingdom and then return. Calling ten of his servants, he gave them ten minas, and said to them, "Engage in business until I come"'" (19:12-13).

Jesus is the nobleman who is about to die, resurrect, ascend to his throne in heaven, and stay there for a while before returning to end world history. In between times, his disciples have kingdom work to do. Just as the nobleman gave his servants a mina each (about three months' wages), Jesus has given his followers all the necessary talents to do their work, and he wants to see a return on his investment. "Engage in business until I come."

It wasn't going to be easy for the servants in the parable, because the nobleman's "citizens hated him and sent a delegation after him, saying, 'We do not want this man to reign over us'" (19:14). The faithful would have to invest while living in a hostile environment that would do everything possible to make them fail.

Jesus invests everything in poor stocks in tough times.

Does he expect much return?

Our Master Checks His Investment 19:15–27

The Master returned and called his servants to give account of their investments. "The first came before him, saying, 'Lord, your mina has made ten minas more.' And he said to him, 'Well done, good servant! Because you have been faithful in a very little, you shall have authority over ten cities'" (19:16–17). From ten minas to ten cities, what a disproportionate reward! Whatever profit the servant gained for the Master, he gained far more for himself.

It went similarly for the five-mina man (19:18–19). But the one-mina man had simply taken the mina he was given and stored it. When he gave it back without any interest, he blamed his inaction on the Master. "I was afraid of you, because you are a severe man. You take what you did not deposit, and reap what you did not sow" (19:21). The Master retorted that if the servant really thought that, the least he could have done was invest the money in the bank and gained a little interest. He therefore took the mina from him and gave it to the ten-mina man (19:22–25).

What we do in this world is determined not only by our view of the end of the world, but also by our view of God. If we view God as harsh and severe, we will do nothing to advance his kingdom. God loses interest on earth, and such unproductive servants lose their heavenly reward.

Jesus is interested in our interest.

Changing Our Story with God's Story

A right view of the end times generates productive and rewarding times, and a rich view of God produces a rich return on investment.

Summary: What is the proper and productive way to view the end times? The most productive eschatology is the right eschatology. Therefore, *aggressively invest your talents for God's kingdom, expecting a disproportionate reward from our rich God.*

Question: What gifts, opportunities, and resources has God given you, and how are you using them?

Prayer: My Good Master, you have given me talents and called me to engage in kingdom business. Therefore, show me what, where, and how to invest these gifts for your honor and glory.

Our perfect Savior had perfect pleasure in his perfect salvation.

Hear
God's Story

Change
Your Story

Tell
the Story

Change
Others' Stories

37

Emotional Theology

LUKE 19:28-46

Jesus is the most emotional person who ever lived. He's had greater joy than anyone ever, greater sorrow than anyone ever, and greater anger than anyone ever. If we want to be like Christ, we have to feel like Christ. We have to ask not only "What would Jesus do?" but "What would Jesus feel?"

So, how do we feel like Jesus? In Luke 19:28-44 we learn from Jesus how to feel like Jesus as he swings from maximum joy to maximum sorrow to maximum anger. Let's feel what he felt and understand why.

Jesus Rejoices in Salvation 19:28-40

As Jesus approached Jerusalem, he sent two disciples ahead to Bethany to find a colt and bring it to him (19:28-32). The people made a carpet of cloaks for him to ride on (19:33-36), and as he descended the Mount of Olives into Jerusalem, "the whole multitude of his disciples began to rejoice and praise God with a loud voice for all the mighty works that they had seen, saying, 'Blessed is the King who comes in the name of the Lord! Peace in heaven and glory in the highest!'" (19:37-38).

When the Pharisees saw how happy Jesus and his disciples were, they said to Jesus, "Teacher, rebuke your disciples" (19:39). But he responded, "I tell you, if these were silent, the very stones would cry out" (19:40). Jesus was enjoying the joy that his joyful people had in him and the salvation he was bringing. No Pharisee was going to spoil this party.

Our perfect Savior had perfect pleasure in his perfect salvation.

Was Jesus happy all the time?
No, he also had perfect sadness at the perfect time for the perfect reason.

Jesus Weeps Over Destruction 19:41–44

Jesus's mood changed dramatically as he switched suddenly from laughing to crying. Why? "When he drew near and saw the city, he wept over it, saying, 'Would that you, even you, had known on this day the things that make for peace! But now they are hidden from your eyes'" (19:41–42). Jesus wept because unrepentant and unbelieving Jerusalem was missing out on massive blessing. But more than that, he wept because he saw that Jerusalem would be judged with destruction because they rejected the visiting Savior (19:43–44). Jesus took no pleasure in the death of the wicked but sobbed over their impending slaughter.

No one had greater joy in salvation or greater grief in condemnation.

What about anger? Surely gentle Jesus, meek and mild, was never angry.

Jesus Rages against Corruption 19:45–46

For some of us, "Be angry and do not sin" (Eph. 4:26) is the hardest commandment in the Bible to keep. But Jesus kept it perfectly. No one was angrier, yet no one was holier. He was angry at the right things at the right time and in the right way. Nothing made him angrier than the religious corruption he saw in the temple. "He entered the temple and began to drive out those who sold, saying to them, 'It is written, "My house shall be a house of prayer," but you have made it a den of robbers'" (19:45–46). They were stealing from God in the house of the giving God.

We can sin both in anger and by not being angry.

Changing Our Story with God's Story

Feeling the greatest joy over salvation, the greatest sorrow over destruction, and the greatest rage against corruption is to be like Christ. Christ's Story calls us to maximum joy in the salvation of sinners, maximum sorrow in the condemnation of sinners, and maximum anger over the conning of sinners. None of us has ever rejoiced enough in our Savior, wept enough over sinners, or raged enough over exploitation. We need and want more of each of these feelings. But ultimately our hope isn't in our feelings but in Christ's feelings. His flawless feelings cover our faulty feelings.

Summary: How do we feel like Jesus? *Christlikeness is feeling the right feelings at the right time to the right degree for the right reasons.*

Question: How can you rejoice better, weep better, and rage better?

Prayer: I worship you, Lord Jesus, as the perfect feeler, and pray for more of your perfect passions of perfect joy, sorrow, and anger in my life.

Painful giving is pleasing giving.

 Hear God's Story | Change Your Story | Tell the Story | Change Others' Stories

38

Big Gratitude for a Small Gift

LUKE 21:1-4

How often have you thought, "What's the point in giving anything to the Lord when I have so little to give?" We look around and see how much others can give and get discouraged at our pitiful pittance. The church treasurer gives us our end-of-year statement, and we think, "Well, that did next to nothing." But *how does Jesus view our giving*? He has a most encouraging answer for us in Luke 21:1–4.

Jesus Welcomes Small Gifts 21:1-2

In the previous verses, Jesus warned his followers about religious leaders who "like to walk around in long robes, and love greetings in the marketplaces and the best seats in the synagogues and the places of honor at feasts, who devour widows' houses and for a pretense make long prayers. They will receive the greater condemnation" (20:46–47). These were religious show-offs who did everything to get attention and applause.

"Jesus looked up and saw the rich putting their gifts into the offering box" (21:1). He watched them swaggering up to the collection boxes in the temple, making sure everyone saw how much they were giving.

But, while everyone else was admiring these arrogant actors, Jesus's eyes were elsewhere. "He saw a poor widow put in two small copper coins" (21:2). No one else saw this, but Jesus did. No one went home talking about this destitute widow, but Jesus did. Little did she know that Jesus would preserve her little gift forever in his word. Jesus relishes and revels in the smallest gift.

Small gifts are seen gifts.

How much then should I give?

Jesus Enjoys Sacrificial Gifts 21:3–4

One day, a dad saw his son counting out how much savings he had in his piggy bank. He was saving up for a new football. "Son, there's been a terrible earthquake in Haiti and lots of children have lost everything. Would you like to give some of your savings to help these poor children?" His son thought for a while, gathered up all his coins and said, "Dad, I want to give it all to these suffering boys and girls. It's only $3.57, but it might help even one child for at least one day."

Deeply moved, the dad was inspired to ask other family members for donations and eventually collected over three thousand dollars. Everyone gave more than his son, but no one gave more than his son. Everyone else who gave didn't notice even the smallest dent in their bank balances, but his son had no bank balance left.

Jesus commended the poor widow because, like this little boy, she gave little but she gave all. "Truly, I tell you, this poor widow has put in more than all of them. For they all contributed out of their abundance, but she out of her poverty put in all she had to live on" (21:3–4). She gave all she had left to live on to God and depended on God to provide for her. Her two small copper coins spoke of one big act of trust.

Painful giving is pleasing giving.

Changing Our Story with God's Story

Even if we give only a dollar, Jesus compassionately records the amount and weighs the pain. Indeed, when Jesus assesses our annual giving, he's not so much calculating the gain to the church but the loss to the giver. Our pain is our gratitude. Our pain is his pleasure. And as we feel that pain of giving, we are reminded of Jesus's sacrificial giving. *Jesus gave it all, all to him I owe.*

Summary: How does Jesus view our limited giving? *Keep giving because Jesus welcomes small gifts and enjoys sacrificial gifts.*

Question: How does this change how much you give to the Lord, and how you give to the Lord?

Prayer: Generous God, you gave all, even sacrificing your Son to enrich me. Therefore, help me to give back to you sacrificially.

Jesus was ground and squeezed for us.

39

A Beautiful Host and His Ugly Guests

LUKE 22:14-30

The Lord's Table can be intimidating rather than inviting. Hearing Paul's warnings in 1 Corinthians 11:27–32 about eating and drinking there in an unworthy manner or without discerning the Lord's body, we are scared away from taking our seats with joy. *How can we make the Lord's Table more inviting than intimidating?* In Luke 22:14–30 Jesus fills every seat with two truths.

The Lord's Table Has a Beautiful Host 22:14-20

On the eve of his death, Jesus "reclined at table, and the apostles with him" (22:14). This is one of the most staggering statements in all of Scripture. Knowing that in a few hours he would be crucified by people and abandoned by God, he laid back and relaxed with his disciples. Anyone else would have been incapacitated with terror.

Even more remarkably, he said, "I have earnestly desired to eat this Passover with you before I suffer" (22:15). He's not doing this reluctantly or hesitantly but with enthusiasm and excitement. He's lived and longed for this moment when he would replace the Passover by becoming the Passover. He even thanks God for this (22:17).

Just as the Passover was instituted to remind Israel of God's salvation, Jesus institutes a supper of bread and wine to remind his disciples of his beautiful salvation. "And he took bread, and when he had given thanks, he broke it and gave it to them, saying, 'This is my body, which is given for you. Do this in remembrance of me.' And likewise the cup after they had eaten, saying, 'This cup that is poured out for you is the new covenant in my blood'" (22:19–20).

They would never look at bread and wine the same way again. Broken bread would now be his broken body, and poured wine would be his streaming blood.

Jesus was ground and squeezed for us.

What a beautifully welcoming sight, sound, and taste.
But what are the guests like?

The Lord's Table Has Ugly Guests 22:21–30

This beautiful table has some ugly guests. One of them is about to deface and destroy the beautiful host. "But behold, the hand of him who betrays me is with me on the table. For the Son of Man goes as it has been determined, but woe to that man by whom he is betrayed!" (22:21–22). He's warning Judas of his end.

Within earshot of the servant of servants, others are arguing about who is the greatest (22:24). He who put himself last and least is watching sinners argue about who is first and most. But he doesn't pull the tablecloth off and overturn the table. Instead, he gently coaches them away from this pagan competition toward Christlike competition.

In the former the greatest are served; in the latter the servants are great. "Let the greatest among you become as the youngest, and the leader as one who serves. For who is the greater, one who reclines at table or one who serves? Is it not the one who reclines at table? But I am among you as the one who serves" (22:26–27).

Some ugly guests, right? Hate and pride occupy most of the seats. But that actually encourages us to take ours.

The Lord's Table is a sinner's table.

Changing Our Story with God's Story

If we need any more encouragement to sit at the Lord's Table with joy and confidence, Jesus points us to the future heavenly table where his ugly guests will not only be beautiful but powerful: "I assign to you, as my Father assigned to me, a kingdom, that you may eat and drink at my table in my kingdom and sit on thrones judging the twelve tribes of Israel" (22:29–30).

Summary: How can we make the Lord's Table more inviting than intimidating? *Use the sight of the beautiful host and his ugly guests to attract you to your seat.*

Question: What keeps you from enjoying the Lord's Table, and how will you use this story to change your story?

Prayer: Beautiful Host, thank you for inviting an ugly sinner like me to your table. Help me to feast on you by faith so that I can enjoy you forever in heaven.

God uses prayer to strengthen us to pray.

40

The Worst Temptation

LUKE 22:39-46

What is the worst temptation? Some say it's sexual temptation. Others say it's pride. Jesus says the worst temptation is fighting against God's plan. The worst temptation was the first temptation in the garden of Eden, and it was also Christ's biggest temptation in the garden of Gethsemane. *What's the best strategy to defeat the worst temptation?* In Luke 22:39-46, Jesus shares his plan for fighting the temptation to fight God's plan.

Pray before Temptation 22:39-40

After administering the Lord's Supper, Jesus knew that what he had pictured was about to become a reality. His body was about to be broken and his blood shed. He therefore went to one of his favorite places for prayer, the Mount of Olives, turned to his disciples and said, "Pray that you may not enter into temptation" (22:40).

What temptation was this? The temptation that was dominating Jesus's mind was the temptation to question, ignore, or reject God's plan for his suffering and death, as we'll see in the next verses. Feeling the heat of this battle and experiencing its agony, he looked with pity on his disciples and said, "Pray that you may not enter into temptation." I know how bad and hard this is, so pray you'll never experience it.

Pray before temptation happens so that temptation will not happen.

But what if it does happen?

Pray in Temptation 22:41-44

No one was ever tempted like Jesus in this area of resisting God's plan. We can feel the heat and hear the artillery of spiritual warfare in his prayer. "Father, if you are willing, remove this cup from me. Nevertheless, not my will, but yours, be done" (22:42). Jesus's human will understandably shrunk from the duty to die such a death in obedience to God, yet by prayer he submitted his will to God.

And what encouragement God sent to his battling Son: "There appeared to him an angel from heaven, strengthening him" (22:43). He then used that strength to pray even more: "Being in agony he prayed more earnestly; and his sweat became like great drops of blood falling down to the ground" (22:44).

God uses prayer to strengthen us to pray.

What should we do when God brings us out of temptation?

Pray after Temptation 22:45-46

Having prayed before temptation and in temptation, Jesus now rises from prayer and says to his sleeping disciples, "Why are you sleeping? Rise and pray that you may not enter into temptation" (22:46). Prayer against the temptation to resist God's providence or fight God's plan is ongoing in the Christian life. It's a constant danger.

Christ's temptation was now over, the battle was won. But he knew his disciples were about to go to the frontline, and he therefore urges them to pray that they not even begin to argue with God's plan.

Sleepy Christians are tempted Christians.

Changing Our Story with God's Story

One of my friends lost a child, and I've never seen anyone engage in such a ferocious spiritual battle to submit to this divine providence. Nothing has challenged his faith in God's plan like this agony.

I know a single Christian woman in her early thirties, and every day of loneliness and solitariness is a battle to submit to God's plan, which is the opposite of hers.

I've had some bitter disappointments in God's providence for me, producing MMA type fights to bring my will into submission to God's. But however hard it can be to accept God's Story as our story, through prayer, we eventually believe we cannot write a better one, submit, and hand over our pen, saying, "Nevertheless, not my will, but your will be done."

Summary: What is the best strategy to defeat the worst temptation? *Pray before, in, and after any temptation to doubt, question, reject, or rebel against God's providence.*

Question: When have you been tempted to fight God's plan for your life, and what helped you defeat the temptation?

Prayer: Perfect Planner, you've planned the large and small print of my life. Help me to always fold and never fight the hand you deal me.

Jesus made hands to hold him.

41

Body Dysmorphic Disorder

LUKE 22:47-53

In a recent Instagram post, Tallulah Willis described her struggles with body dysmorphic disorder. She said she used to punish herself for resembling her dad Bruce Willis instead of looking like her mom Demi Moore.

Body dysmorphic disorder is a mental illness involving obsessive focus on a perceived flaw in appearance. The person often spends hours a day trying to fix a minor or imagined flaw with cosmetics, exercise, and so on, and it's often accompanied by debilitating anxiety, embarrassment, and social isolation.

How should we view our bodies in a healthy and happy way? Let's see how Jesus viewed them in Luke 22:47-53.

Jesus Appeals to Sinful Lips 22:47-48

Having been strengthened by an angel in Gethsemane, Jesus looks up to see the devil coming toward him in the form of Judas and the mob. Judas "drew near to Jesus to kiss him, but Jesus said to him, 'Judas, would you betray the Son of Man with a kiss?'" (22:47–48).

These were lips that had spoken to Jesus and spoken of Jesus, but now were murdering Jesus. These were lips that had affectionately greeted Jesus, but now were treacherously identifying him for crucifixion. While some of us might have punched these lying lips, Jesus spoke the truth to them once more with a last-ditch appeal to Judas's humanity and his conscience: "Judas, are you really going to betray the Son of Man? With a kiss? Do you know who I am? Do you know what you're doing? Do you really want to be remembered for the worst kiss in history?"

Jesus made lips to love him.

What other parts of our bodies is Jesus interested in?

Jesus Heals a Sinful Ear 22:49–51

John's Gospel informs us that Peter angrily sliced off the ear of Malchus, the High Priest's servant (John 18:10). When Jesus picked up the severed ear, he saw an ear that he had designed and made in all its beautiful complexity. As he held the amputated ear, he knew this ear had heard his words in the temple and its surroundings. Yet this was a deaf ear, an ear that refused to listen to the truth.

Despite all this, Jesus lovingly reconnected the ear and powerfully healed it. The last miracle before he was killed, he reached out to sinners like Judas and Malchus with his mercy and grace, to the very end.

Jesus made ears to hear him.

Jesus Disarms Sinful Hands 22:52–53

Having appealed to Judas's lips, and healed Malchus's ear, Jesus then turns to the mob's hands. "Have you come out as against a robber, with swords and clubs? When I was with you day after day in the temple, you did not lay hands on me. But this is your hour, and the power of darkness" (22:52–53).

The giver was treated as a robber, the peacemaker was treated as a terrorist. They came to arrest him with weapons, but he arrested them with his words. He stopped them in their tracks with the facts. "You know I'm a man of peace, so why are you handling me like a man of war? Why take me with violence, when I surrender myself to you with calm?" He's saying, "Drop your unnecessary weapons and embrace your necessary Savior."

Jesus made hands to hold him.

Changing Our Story with God's Story

Our bodies are spoiled by sin, but they are saveable by Jesus. We lay our sinful lips, ears, and hands (and every other body part) at the foot of the crucified Savior for forgiveness. Then, by the mercies of God, we present our bodies as living sacrifices, holy and acceptable to God, which is our spiritual worship (Rom. 12:1). And, ultimately, we look forward to the day when Jesus will transform our lowly body to be like his glorious body (Phil. 3:21).

Summary: How should we view our bodies? *Like Jesus, view your body as sinful but saveable and serviceable.*

Question: Which part of your body is Jesus appealing to, healing, disarming, or calling to serve him?

Prayer: My Maker, I dedicate my entire body to you and your service, holding nothing back, because you didn't hold back yourself.

There were
innumerable reasons
to praise Christ,
but zero reasons
to persecute him.

42

Worst Friends Forever

LUKE 23:8-16

Persecution is puzzling. *Why do people hate Christ and Christians so much?* If there's one thing our divided world is united on, it's hatred of Jesus and his followers. Why? Why do they hate us more than any other religion, more even than the worst criminals? If we could figure it out, it would be somewhat easier to bear. If we could see some reason for their persecution, we would have a reason for our suffering. Why do people hate Christ and Christians so much?

In Luke 23:8-16, we see two enemies become friends in their persecution of Christ. Let's see if we can find some clues to their hellish unity.

Persecutors Look for a Reason to Persecute 23:8-12

The mob had been pressuring Pilate to convict and condemn Christ, but when his questioning failed to elicit any wrongdoing, the coward passed the buck to Herod. "When Herod saw Jesus, he was very glad, for he had long desired to see him, because he had heard about him, and he was hoping to see some sign done by him" (23:8). How then do Herod and the mob treat him?

- They interrogate Jesus. "[Herod] questioned him at some length, but he made no answer" (23:9).
- They accuse Jesus: "The chief priests and the scribes stood by, vehemently accusing him" (23:10).

- They despise Jesus: "Herod with his soldiers treated him with contempt" (23:11).
- They mock Jesus: "[They] mocked him. Then, arraying him in splendid clothing, [Herod] sent him back to Pilate" (23:11).
- They use Jesus: "And Herod and Pilate became friends with each other that very day, for before this they had been at enmity with each other" (23:12). They used Jesus as a political pawn for political gain. It's a friendship made in hell.

They do all this to find a reason for their persecution, or to provoke a reason for their persecution. If they can get Jesus to react badly, then they will have a rational basis for what they want to do.

Persecutors start with an effect, then look for a cause.

So, what reason did they find?

Persecutors Find No Reason to Persecute 23:13–16

What then was the verdict and sentence? Pilate speaks: "You brought me this man as one who was misleading the people. And after examining him before you, behold, I did not find this man guilty of any of your charges against him. Neither did Herod, for he sent him back to us" (23:14–15). The verdict in both Pilate's and Herod's courts was "not guilty."

And the sentence? Pilate announces, "Look, nothing deserving death has been done by him. I will therefore punish and release him." What? Not guilty, therefore I'll punish him? No crime, therefore I'll treat him as a criminal? Do you see how irrational this hatred is? There was zero reason to punish Jesus, yet they punished him. They searched high and low for a reason to punish, found none, and therefore punished him! There was no reason to punish and every reason to praise, yet they chose to punish.

There were innumerable reasons to praise Christ, but zero reasons to persecute him.

Changing Our Story with God's Story

There is no rational reason to persecute Christians. It is irrational, it is unreasonable, it is illogical, it is senseless. The only "reason" is a spiritual one. Persecutors are stirred up by the irrationality of the devil to love irrational darkness and hate rational light. If we can understand that story, it will change our story.

Summary: Why do people hate Christ and Christians so much? *There's no reason for this unreasonableness, therefore follow the reasonableness of Christ in his quiet submission to unreasonableness.*

Question: When have you experienced irrational hatred toward Christ and his followers?

Prayer: My Best Friend Forever, protect me from my worst enemies, or grant me patient submission to their unreasonableness.

Jesus doesn't want our compassion; he wants our confidence.

43

Cry or Die

LUKE 23:27-31

Some people weep for Jesus when they should weep for themselves. I remember when *The Passion of the Christ* was showing, lots of people were coming out of movie theaters crying. When interviewed about it, they were asked if they now believed in Christ. Most said no. When asked if the movie would change their life, again all said versions of "Not really."

What was going on there? *How can people weep over Christ's suffering for sin, but not turn from their sin?* Luke 23:27-31 explains how people can shed tears over Christ's suffering but not shed the sins that caused it.

Jesus Is Confident When Facing Suffering 23:27-28

Pilate caved to the mob and sentenced Jesus to death. As Jesus was led away to be executed, "there followed him a great multitude of the people and of women who were mourning and lamenting for him" (23:27).

No wonder! Just basic humanity would have wept over the grave and fatal injustice done to this good and godly person. But more than natural affection, there was also spiritual affection. He had been a blessing to people's souls and had healed many of them from diseases. Perhaps some also had spiritual understanding mixed in with their tears as they grasped the enormity of seeing the Savior dying in their place for their sins.

Whatever the reason for their tears, Jesus told them to divert them from him to themselves: "But turning to them Jesus said,

'Daughters of Jerusalem, do not weep for me, but weep for your-selves and for your children'" (23:28). "Do not weep for me" was an expression of Christ's confidence in facing execution, death, and burial. He knew the end result would render tears unneces-sary, replacing them with joy in his salvation. "Do not weep for me, because it's a waste of tears. There's nothing to sorrow about and plenty to rejoice about." This was not a rebuke of their tears, but an expression of total faith in his Father's plan. His confidence should cultivate our confidence.

Jesus doesn't want our compassion; he wants our confidence.

I understand Christ's confidence,
but why was he so concerned about the mourners?

Jesus Is Concerned for His Children's Suffering 23:28–31

"Do not weep for me, but weep for yourselves and for your children." Having stopped the multitude's tears for him, he starts them for them-selves. Why? "For behold, the days are coming when they will say, 'Blessed are the barren and the wombs that never bore and the breasts that never nursed!' Then they will begin to say to the mountains, 'Fall on us,' and to the hills, 'Cover us'" (23:29–30). Jesus knew that Israel was going to be judged for rejecting the Messiah, and Jerusalem especially would suffer terribly in the Roman siege forty years later. Many would starve to death in the siege, and others would be captured and killed. Jerusalem , including the temple, would be destroyed.

These tear-filled verses are rounded off with Christ's enigmatic comment: "For if they do these things when the wood is green, what will happen when it is dry?" (23:31). To put it simply, "If Israel judged the green tree of Christ, how will God judge the dry tree of Israel?" Jesus wants us to weep over our spiritual danger and recognize that we need him in our lives as our green tree.

Rejection of the green tree of Jesus will turn us into a dry tree of judgment.

Changing Our Story with God's Story

This story should change our story by making us happier and sadder. We should be happy that Jesus died for our sins, but sad that our sins meant he had to die. And if we shed tears over our sins, we will shed our sins too.

Summary: How can people cry over Christ's suffering for sin, but not turn from their sin? *Cry over your sin as the cause of Christ's suffering, and you'll be changed by Christ's suffering for your sin.*

Question: What sin will you shed today by shedding tears of repentance?

Prayer: Suffering Savior, I confess that my sin caused your suffering. Thank you for suffering not just to move me, but to save me and change me.

The nails nail
salvation by works.

44

What Happens the Moment after Death?

LUKE 23:39-43

What happens the second after we die? That question troubles some Christians. That's understandable, because it's an experience we've never had before and there's no one we can ask about it either. We leave behind all that's known and familiar and enter the unknown and unfamiliar. But is it? Thankfully, in Luke 23:39–43, Jesus gives us a glimpse into that foreign world, and although he doesn't answer all our questions, he answers them sufficiently to look ahead to that moment with joy not fear.

Jesus Convicts 23:39-41

Matthew reported that the men crucified with Christ were violent robbers (Matt. 27:44). Crucifixion implies that they were either serious repeat offenders or else they had killed someone during the robbery. We get an insight into how callous their hearts were from the one thief who, even to the end, "railed at [Christ], saying, 'Are you not the Christ? Save yourself and us!'" (Luke 23:39). These were tough, hardened criminals.

But one heart is changing. While one thief is yelling at Jesus, the other rebukes him, saying, "Do you not fear God, since you are under the same sentence of condemnation? And we indeed justly, for we are receiving the due reward of our deeds; but this man has done nothing wrong" (23:40–41). Seeing Jesus close up, this thief recognizes Christ's perfection and his own just condemnation.

A court's conviction condemns, but Christ's conviction saves.

Conviction is one thing, but what about conversion?

Jesus Converts 23:42

Having rebuked his partner in crime, the repentant thief turns to Jesus and prays, maybe for the first time: "Jesus, remember me when you come into your kingdom" (23:42). This must be one of the greatest acts of faith in world history. Jesus looks about as far from a king as anyone could at this point. He had been beaten, bruised, bloodied, nailed to the cross, crowned with thorns, and hoisted naked before a cursing mocking crowd. But whatever the thief saw with his eyes, he saw a king by faith.

And what a prayer! He asked for little—but he asked for everything. "Among the millions and millions of your subjects, please take a moment to think about me and take care of me, would you?" Notice that the thief says, "*When* you come into your kingdom." There's no *if*; it's *when*. This is a converted man who realized he could do nothing to save himself.

The nails nail salvation by works.

Does Jesus just leave him hanging?

Jesus Comforts 23:43

With one of his last breaths, Jesus turns to his new son and says, "Truly, I say to you, today you will be with me in paradise" (23:43). As soon as any and every believer dies, they are with Christ in paradise. There's no purgatory, only paradise.

What do you think were the most precious words to the thief in this promise? *Today* was valuable; *paradise* was prized; but *with me* was priceless. "You will be with me." From with him on the cross to with him in paradise. All the thief wanted was to be remembered by Jesus, but he got far more. He got "with Jesus." What a comfort!

Jesus does not just remember us; he's with us forever.

Changing Our Story with God's Story

In less than a blink of the eye, the dying believer is with Jesus in heaven. We will have no delays, no detours, no stops, no lines. As soon as we die, we are in paradise with Jesus. Pray this simple prayer today and remove fear now and forever: "King Jesus, remember me." That's the password to paradise.

Summary: What happens the moment after we die? *There's not a tick or a tock between pain here and paradise there.*

Questions: How does this death story change your life story? How can you use it to change someone else's life story, death story, and eternity story?

Prayer: King Jesus, among the millions and millions of your subjects and activities, please take a moment to think about me, take care of me, and bring me to your kingdom when I die.

The darkest moment in history was also the brightest moment in history.

45

The Darkest and Brightest Moment in History

LUKE 23:44–49

All of us go through dark times in our lives. Whether long or short, rare or common, a one-off or repeated, we endure scarily dark times of despair and despondency. *How do we find light in the darkness?* Let's see how Luke found the brightest light in the darkest moment of human history in Luke 23:44–49.

Jesus's Death Was the Darkest Moment in History 23:44–45

As life drained from Jesus, light disappeared from the world. "It was now about the sixth hour, and there was darkness over the whole land until the ninth hour, while the sun's light failed" (23:44–45). It was midnight at midday as a miraculous but terrible darkness enveloped Calvary.

How far did this darkness extend? Luke explains that *the sun's light failed*, which means darkness swallowed the whole world. If someone had been looking from outer space, he would have seen the sun and planet earth in darkness, a darkness that lasted from noon to three. God marked the worst moment in history with the blackest darkness in history.[1]

God turned off the lights because humanity turned off the Light.

---

1 Some commentators take the view that this was a local (not worldwide) and limited darkness (not pitch black). Whatever the area or depth of the darkness, it was clearly understood as miraculous by the observers.

Was there any bright side to this dark scene?

Jesus's Death Was the Brightest Moment in History 23:45–49

God gives us hints that this darkest moment in the world may yet lighten the whole world.

First, "the curtain of the temple was torn in two" (23:45). The physical barrier of the big thick curtain that separated sinners from the temple's most holy place was ripped from top to bottom by an invisible hand. Christ's ripped flesh ripped the curtain of sin from top to bottom and opened full access to God. Light in the darkness.

Second, "Jesus, calling out with a loud voice, said, 'Father, into your hands I commit my spirit!' And having said this he breathed his last" (23:46). Jesus entrusted his soul to God, making clear that no one was taking his life from him, but he was laying it down of his own volition (John 10:18). In full control of himself and of events to the end, he died not as a passive victim but as an active victor. Light in the darkness.

Third, "when the centurion saw what had taken place, he praised God, saying, 'Certainly this man was innocent!'" (23:47). While plunged into darkness, one of the leading crucifiers saw the light. Risking his own life by critiquing Roman injustice and by praising God instead of Caesar, his confession of Christ's innocence and his guilt shone brightly in the darkness.

Fourth, "all the crowds that had assembled for this spectacle, when they saw what had taken place, returned home beating their breasts" (23:48). Just a few hours earlier, they had been a baying mob crying out for Christ's death. Now, convicted of their sin, they were crying over Christ's death. Light in the darkness.

These four lights in the darkness are the first glimmers of the life-giving light that would soon gleam throughout the globe by the gospel turning the worst moment in history into the best.

The darkest moment in history was also the brightest moment in history.

Changing Our Story with God's Story

If Jesus can turn the darkest moment in human history into the brightest, then he can turn our darkest moments into light as well.

Summary: How do we find light in the darkness? *Find light in the darkness by finding Jesus in the darkness.*

Question: How can you share your darkness-to-light experience with someone else who is still in the darkness?

Prayer: Light-Giver, shine your light in me and through me to enlighten my dark soul and this dark world.

Jesus gave his body for our bodies.

46

Body Language

LUKE 23:50-56

Our bodies speak even when our mouths don't. Body language is a type of nonverbal communication in which physical behaviors (e.g., posture, eye movement, touch, facial expressions) express our thoughts and convey information. Although most of us learn how to use and understand this language to some extent, some experts are able to interpret the slightest movements, even tiny twitches.

What is your body saying to those around you? Specifically, *what message does your body communicate about the gospel?* In Luke 23:50-56, we hear believers' bodies speaking about Jesus's body. Let's listen to their message.

Our Bodies Are for Jesus 23:50-52

Joseph of Arimathea's body was devoted to the Lord. "Now there was a man named Joseph, from the Jewish town of Arimathea. He was a member of the council, a good and righteous man . . . and he was looking for the kingdom of God" (23:50-51). Joseph's body language was consistent with his lip language. He talked the talk and walked the walk. He knew what was good and righteous and practiced it. His posture was future oriented as his eyes looked eagerly for the coming of God's kingdom.

Joseph risked his body for the Lord. "He was a member of the council . . . who had not consented to their decision and action" (23:51). Joseph was a member of the Jewish court that had condemned Jesus to death but, as far as we know, he was the only dissenter to that decision. What courage it must have taken to stand up to the baying mob and the most powerful men and oppose their determination to crucify an innocent man. He knew he was taking his life in his hands but could not sit still in the face of such evil. He stood up and stood against them.

Having risked his body for the living Christ, he then risked his body for the dead Christ. "This man went to Pilate and asked for the body of Jesus" (23:52). Again, it took stunning courage to associate with Jesus and ask for the body of someone who had been cursed by God and man.

Jesus gave us bodies to give to him.

What did Joseph's treatment of Jesus's body communicate?

Jesus's Body Is for Us 23:53–56

We see how precious Jesus's body was to Joseph by the way he cared for it. "He took it down [from the cross] and wrapped it in a linen shroud and laid him in a tomb cut in stone, where no one had ever yet been laid" (23:53). It's a beautiful scene of care and affection for Christ's abandoned body.

We also hear body language from some of the women who loved Jesus. "The women who had come with him from Galilee followed and saw the tomb and how his body was laid. Then they returned and prepared spices and ointments" (23:55–56). Again, without saying a word, their bodies spoke eloquently of how much they valued Christ's macerated body.

Both Joseph and the women expressed their faith in Christ's body given for their bodies. Even time added its voice as "on the Sabbath they rested according to the commandment" (23:56). Christ's resting body had purchased rest for their bodies.

Jesus gave his body for our bodies.

Changing Our Story with God's Story

Whether we are called to sacrifice our bodies for Christ or love the body of Christ, may our bodies speak loudly and clearly of Christ. May this story about Joseph's body and Christ's body change the story of our body.

Summary: What message does your body communicate about the gospel? *Use your whole body to speak of Christ's body to everybody.*

Question: How can you speak of Christ through your body today?

Prayer: Creator of My Body, I present my body to you and thank you for presenting Christ's body to me.

Remembering is better than forgetting, but witnessing is better than wavering.

47

Remember to Respond

LUKE 24:1-12

Memorial Day in the USA is a day to remind ourselves and others of the sacrifices of our military. It's a day not just to remember the ultimate sacrifices of those who have served but to respond with sacrifice and service in our own lives. We remember to respond.

Christ's resurrection is also for remembering and responding. *How do we remember and respond to Christ's resurrection?* When we remember it constantly, we will react to it positively, as the women did in Luke 24:1-12.

We Remember the Resurrection 24:1-8

Having prepared burial spices Saturday evening, on Sunday "at early dawn, [the women] went to the tomb, taking the spices they had prepared" (24:1). When they arrived, they were met with three surprises. First, "they found the stone rolled away from the tomb" (24:2); second, "when they went in they did not find the body of the Lord Jesus" (24:3); and third, "while they were perplexed about this, behold, two men stood by them in dazzling apparel" (24:4). No wonder "they were frightened and bowed their faces to the ground" (24:5).

As they lay prostrate in the tomb, the dusty darkness filled with blinding light, the two men asked them: "Why do you seek the living among the dead? He is not here, but has risen" (24:5-6). World history and our personal history just changed in a handful of words.

Sensing the turmoil and tumult in their minds and hearts, the two angels reminded the women of what they had forgotten: "'Remember how he told you, while he was still in Galilee, that the Son of Man must be delivered into the hands of sinful men and be crucified and on the third day rise.' And they remembered his words" (24:6–8).

Remember Christ's resurrection to remember your resurrection.

How did people respond to the news of Christ's resurrection?

We React to the Resurrection 24:9–12

Remembering the resurrection is better than forgetting it, but we're to do more than remember it. We are to react and respond to it. It's not a historical fact for us to memorize, but a historical fact that should revolutionize us. So how did people respond to the resurrection?

The women witnessed. "Returning from the tomb they told all these things to the eleven and to all the rest. Now it was Mary Magdalene and Joanna and Mary the mother of James and the other women with them who told these things to the apostles" (24:9–10).

The disciples doubted. "These words seemed to them an idle tale, and they did not believe them" (24:11).

Peter investigated. He wasn't an immediate witness like the women or a skeptical doubter like the rest of the disciples. Instead, he probed and examined the evidence. "Peter rose and ran to the tomb; stooping and looking in, he saw the linen cloths by themselves; and he went home marveling at what had happened" (24:12).

Remembering is better than forgetting, but witnessing is better than wavering.

Changing Our Story with God's Story

Today we have not only the predictions of the resurrection to remember, but the actual resurrection to remember. How much better should our memories and reactions be than the women and the disciples! The women witnessed, the disciples wavered, and Peter wondered. Let's move from wavering to wondering to witnessing.

Summary: How do we remember and respond to Christ's resurrection? *Remember the resurrection constantly to react to it positively.*

Question: How will you remember the resurrection more and respond to it better?

Prayer: Resurrected Lord, remind me of your sacrifice, service, and resurrection so that I may be a joyful witness to the resurrection and be resurrected with joy.

Admission to truth begins with admission of error.

48

Spiritual Heartburn

LUKE 24:13-35

"What's the Old Testament all about?" Ever asked that question? I did, many times, over many years. I'd been raised in church, gone to seminary, been a pastor for some years, and preached Old Testament sermons. Yet, I was still puzzled: "What's the Old Testament all about? Why is it in the Bible? What's the point of it when there's no gospel and no Jesus in it?"

But one day, the New Testament gave me the password to the Old Testament, and I want to share it with you (as long as you promise to share the password with others). Are you ready? Here it is—Luke 24:13-35. This password begins with an admission of folly and ignorance.

We Are Foolish and Ignorant 24:13-26

On the same Sunday Christ rose from the dead, he joined two of his disciples traveling from Jerusalem to Emmaus. They were commiserating with one another about Christ's death and defeat. Having patiently listened to their story of disappointed hopes and depressed spirits, Christ then intervened with a rebuke of their foolish ignorance and unbelief. "O foolish ones, and slow of heart to believe all that the prophets have spoken! Was it not necessary that the Christ should suffer these things and enter into his glory?" (24:25-26).

Jesus told them that their account of Christ's life and death exactly matched the predictions of the Old Testament prophets. Had they believed them, they would have expected suffering to precede glory, defeat to come before triumph.

Admission to truth begins with admission of error.

So, did he leave them in foolish ignorance?
No, he gave them a full interpretation.

We Need a Full Interpretation 24:27

Having critiqued their distorted perspective, Jesus then viewed the same events from a divine perspective. "And beginning with Moses and all the Prophets, he interpreted to them in all the Scriptures the things concerning himself" (24:27).

The title of Christ's Old Testament sermon was "The Things Concerning Himself." It had two main points: Christ's sufferings and Christ's glory. Notice three stages of development in his points: "beginning at Moses," he goes on to "all the Prophets," and then expands into "all the Scriptures" (24:27). That's a big text and a long sermon!

The New interprets the Old, and the Old interprets the New.

He opened the Scriptures. Did that open their eyes?

We Are Given Faith's Insight 24:28–35

When it looked as if Jesus was about to part from them on the outskirts of Emmaus, the disciples constrained him to stay with them and continue the Bible study. When they sat down to eat, Jesus "took the bread, and blessed and broke it and gave it to them. And their eyes were opened, and they recognized him. And he vanished from their sight" (24:30–31).

In addition to opening up the Scriptures to them, Christ opened the temporarily shut eyes of their faith, and then opened their hearts.

Turning to one another, the two disciples exclaimed, "Did not our hearts burn within us while he talked to us on the road, while he opened to us the Scriptures?" (24:32). They immediately returned to Jerusalem and told the other disciples, "The Lord has risen indeed" (24:34).

Jesus opens Scripture, eyes, hearts, and mouths.

Changing Our Story with God's Story

My "Road to Emmaus" moment came when I was reading *According to Plan: The Unfolding Revelation of God in the Bible* by Graeme Goldsworthy. Explaining this passage, he wrote: "We do not start at Genesis 1 and work our way forward until we discover where it is all leading. Rather we first come to Christ, and he directs us to study the Old Testament in the light of the gospel."[1] Suddenly the lights turned on and my heart began to burn as God's Story opened, my eyes opened, and my heart opened and began to burn. May God's whole Story change you wholly too.

Summary: What's the Old Testament all about? Jesus's emphatic answer is "Me! Me! Me!" *Ask Christ to use the password of Luke 24 to open up the Old Testament story and thereby change our story with his Story.*

Question: What do you need God to open? The Bible, your eyes, your heart, or your mouth?

Prayer: You are the God who opens. Open the word, my eyes, and my heart to Jesus, so that I may have blessed spiritual heartburn to share with others.

1   Graeme Goldsworthy, *According to Plan: The Unfolding Revelation of God in the Bible* (Downers Grove, IL: InterVarsity Press, 1991), 55.

Jesus is not too good to be true; he's too good and too true.

49

Almost Too Good to Be True

LUKE 24:36-43

What do we do with our doubts? As a young Christian, I did not see any place for apologetics. The idea of presenting proofs for our faith was the opposite of faith, I thought. My "apologetic" was, "Just believe what God says. That's faith."

However, as I grew from baby faith to toddler faith, I began to see that God graciously and gently uses evidences, reasons, and proofs to bring people to faith and to strengthen doubting faith. There's no greater proof of that than Jesus's first appearance to all his disciples in Luke 24:36-43.

Jesus Gives Peace to the Anxious 24:36-38

What were Jesus's first words to the disciples after his resurrection? "Peace to you" (24:36). We might have expected something like, "Where were you all?" or "Why did you all run away?" or "Some friends you are!" or something along these lines. After all, they all forsook him and fled when Jesus was at his lowest point. The last time Jesus saw them, it was their backs he saw as they skulked and sprinted away from the cross.

But the first words he spoke were the last words they expected: "Peace to you." While they were discussing the first reports of Christ's resurrection, "Jesus himself stood among them, and said to them, 'Peace to you!'" (24:36).

Even before that, their anxiety levels were probably rising. Although they wanted to see Jesus again, they were also afraid to see him again. Would he want to see them again? That's why Jesus sought to allay all their fears from the first word he spoke: "Peace." He had not come to pick a fight, to right wrongs, to rebuke, to condemn, but to give peace. What a perfect first word, given that he had just secured peace on the cross and that there was a brewing storm of anxiety in their hearts.

Look at the various words diagnosing the state of their hearts: "But they were startled and frightened and thought they saw a spirit" (24:37). "Why are you troubled, and why do doubts arise in your hearts?" (24:38). "They still disbelieved for joy" (24:41). He saw panic, panic, panic, and therefore gave peace, peace, peace.

When we panic, Jesus gives peace.

But anxiety wasn't their only problem, was it?
No, they were also skeptical.

Jesus Gives Proof to Doubters 24:37–43

The disciples thought Jesus was just a ghost (24:37). He therefore challenges their unbelief: "'Why do doubts arise in your hearts? See my hands and my feet, that it is I myself. Touch me, and see. For a spirit does not have flesh and bones as you see that I have.' And when he had said this, he showed them his hands and his feet" (24:38–40). He not only urged them to look at his hands and feet, bearing the scars of Calvary, he also compelled them to touch him. "See me and touch me," he pleaded.

The result? "They still disbelieved for joy and were marveling" (24:41). Joy was beginning to replace anxiety, but doubt was still stronger than faith. It was almost too good to be true.

Instead of giving up on them, though, he pities them and asks, "'Have you anything here to eat?' They gave him a piece of broiled fish, and he took it and ate before them" (24:41–43). He was saying, "Ghosts don't eat! I'm real, I'm physical, I'm flesh and blood, this is my body broken for you." He's desperate for them to believe for joy rather than disbelieve for joy. "I'm not too good to be true. I am too good and too true!"

Jesus is not too good to be true; he's too good and too true.

Changing Our Story with God's Story

If we're anxious and/or doubting, Jesus can give peace and proof. But Jesus also uses us to change others' stories from fear to peace, and from doubt to proof. Jesus gives us peace and proof so that we can give others peace and proof.

Summary: What do we do with our doubts? *Ask Jesus to give peace through proof.*

Question: To whom can you give proof and peace today?

Prayer: God of Peace, I know I should simply believe, but doubt and fear are running riot and ruining my peace. Therefore, give me peace through proof.

God lifted Jesus to
change our story,
and we lift Jesus to
change other stories.

50

Seven Lifts

LUKE 24:44-53

Don't you just hate movies that end on a low note? They offer such a disappointing anticlimax, leaving us feeling we just wasted our time to depress ourselves. Stories, though, that build toward a wonderful climax strike a high note and leave us feeling inspired and hopeful.

So, how does the story of Jesus end, and what's the effect upon us? The previous forty-nine devotional studies have built up our hopes of an exhilarating ending to Luke's Gospel. Will our hopes of a high note be fulfilled or frustrated? Let's turn to Luke 24:44-53 and soar.

God Lifted Jesus Up 24:44-51

Having convinced the disciples that he was not just a ghost but was real flesh and blood, Jesus then turned their attention to the Scriptures. "He said to them, 'These are my words that I spoke to you while I was still with you, that everything written about me in the Law of Moses and the Prophets and the Psalms must be fulfilled'" (24:44-45). Each Old Testament book lifted up the expected Messiah, and Jesus perfectly fulfilled all these expectations.

"Then he opened their minds to understand the Scriptures, and said to them, 'Thus it is written, that the Christ should suffer and on the third day rise from the dead'" (24:45-46). Having been lifted up in fulfilling the Old Testament, he was then lifted up in his resurrection from the dead.

Going forward, the proclamation of the gospel lifts Christ's name even higher, further, and longer. "Repentance for the forgiveness of sins should be proclaimed in his name to all nations, beginning from Jerusalem. You are witnesses of these things" (24:47–48).

And to help them raise Christ as high as possible, Jesus promises, "Behold, I am sending the promise of my Father upon you. But stay in the city until you are clothed with power from on high" (24:49). Power from on high will help them lift Jesus high.

The fifth and final lift of God came with the ascension of Christ to heaven. "And he led them out as far as Bethany, and lifting up his hands he blessed them. While he blessed them, he parted from them and was carried up into heaven" (24:50–51).

God lifted Jesus up, up, up, up, up, and away.

So what should we do?

We Lift Jesus Up 24:52-53

Inspired by this climactic high point in Jesus's story, Christ's story-tellers continued to elevate Christ higher and higher in response. They lifted up their voices in joyful praise of Jesus and lifted up God in public witness to Jesus. "And they worshiped him and returned to Jerusalem with great joy, and were continually in the temple blessing God" (24:52–53).

The disciples kept the momentum going. God had lifted Jesus five times, and they added two other steps to this elevation in their desire to exalt the StoryChanger and become storychangers themselves.

God lifted Jesus to change our story, and we lift Jesus to change other stories.

Changing Our Story with God's Story

In a world where people lift up themselves and their stories, Jesus calls us to lift him and his Story. That's our greatest joy, isn't it? We get to join with God in his desire and determination to exalt Jesus.

We destroy our story if we exalt our story, but we make our story if we raise his Story. Jesus commissions us, as he commissioned his disciples, to allow his Story to change our stories, and then tell his Story to others so that it changes their stories. There's no higher note and no higher climax.

Summary: How does the Story of Jesus end and what's the effect upon us? *Jesus's Story doesn't end because, inspired by God's raising of Jesus, we continue to raise him with our lips and lives.*

Question: How will you lift Jesus up today?

Prayer: Most High God, you have exalted Jesus. Help me to join you in this by lifting up Jesus so that his mission and mercy continue to change my story and others' stories.

TheStoryChanger.life

To keep changing your story with God's Story, visit www.thestory changer.life for the latest news about more StoryChanger devotionals, to sign up for the StoryChanger newsletter, and to subscribe to *The StoryChanger* podcast.

How Jesus Changes *Our* Story with *His* Story

The StoryChanger
How God Rewrites Our Story by Inviting Us into His

David Murray   An Introduction

David Murray introduces readers to the StoryChanger, Jesus Christ—the only one who can rewrite human stories with his better Story—directing them to the stories of individuals in Scripture to see how their own messy stories can be transformed into stories worth telling.

For more information, visit **crossway.org**.